# NEW HARMONIC DEVICES

# EW HARMONIC DEVICES

## A TREATISE ON MODERN HARMONIC PROBLEMS

*By*

HORACE ALDEN MILLER

2.00

## OLIVER DITSON COMPANY

THEODORE PRESSER CO., DISTRIBUTORS
1712 Chestnut Street          Philadelphia

MADE IN U.S.A.

# PREFACE

This book is intended as an aid for advanced students who may wish to acquire facility in writing in a modern style. Particular emphasis has been placed on the eleventh and thirteenth as workable chord members, the whole-tone harmonies and chord building by superimposed fourths. So little information is available along these lines that this lack would seem an adequate reason for the appearance of this book.

Included are brief chapters on polytonality and atonalism, processes that are in the making and therefore difficult of comprehension. Few realize that the methods of the modern writer are markedly dissimilar to those of the classic composers. The figured bass is an impossibility with the new methods; chords are frequently built from the center outward, and even downward from the highest note; so it is evident that musicians should be made aware of such processes.

Some erudite theorist has declared that theorists in general are at least fifty years behind the times; so it is necessary, if we are to maintain our proper self-respect, that we apply ourselves to present-day needs.

The general opinion is that theorists must always move in the rear of practice; but one can scarcely conceive of any theorist being able to keep pace with the present-day composer, so some of the seeming revolutionary methods in this book will be found moderate by the would-be critic when he investigates some of the modern music.

The author realizes, however, that there will naturally be a division of opinion on many problems of modern music, and it is important that some discussions be carried on to clear the academic atmosphere. Arnold Schönberg (in his

*Treatise on Harmony*) writes of the teacher that "he is not the infallible, the man who knows everything and never errs, but the indefatigable who is forever seeking and sometimes rewarded by finding."

The author is indebted to the following authorities for valuable hints: A. Eaglefield Hull, Renè Lenormand, C. H. Kitson, George Dyson, Arnold Schönberg, Egon Wellesz, Alfredo Casella, Arthur Heacox, F. J. Lehmann, Adolph Weidig, Arthur Olaf Anderson, Felix Borowski, Gustav Holst, and Herbert Howells.

HORACE ALDEN MILLER

Cornell College
Mount Vernon, Iowa

# ACKNOWLEDGMENTS

The author's best thanks are due to the following publishers for their kind permission to reproduce excerpts from
their copyright works:

Murdock, Murdock & Co.

Rouart, Lerolle & Cie

Maurice Senart

A. Durand & Fils

Arthur P. Schmidt Co.

G. Schirmer, Inc.

Carl Fischer, Inc.

C. C. Birchard & Co.

G. Ricordi & Co.

Publishers of Edition Peters

Boosey & Co.

Novello & Co., Ltd.

J. & W. Chester, Ltd.

Elkin & Co., Ltd.

Schott & Co.

Rob. Forberg

J. Curwen & Sons, Ltd.

Publishers of Universal Edition

Winthrop Rogers, Ltd.

Swan & Co.

Oxford University Press

A. Forlivesi & C.

# CONTENTS

# INTRODUCTION

## (HARMONY IN RETROSPECT)

It is needless to say that one who attacks the problem of modern harmony with the intention of rationalizing it will perhaps be considered presumptuous. Doubtless all theory teachers at times have notions about certain problems that are worthy of attention. But most teachers are not bold enough to broach these solutions, even if they have a vehicle of expression. The author, fortified by constant research and consultation with various musicians, is presuming to present some of these problems and their solutions in an endeavor to justify, and even here and there to indicate, a modest prognostication of future harmonies. If it is true that the theorist should "move behind practice," there is no need of moving fifty years behind. As to the future, a certain estimate may be conjectured from the trend of the times. "Inconsistency is the despair of those lovers of an art who are not unsympathetic to reform, for the unravelling of confused issues is a thankless task. . . . . Criticism should be most tireless when reformers are most aggressive . . . . Not only must tradition itself be examined without prejudice, but reform must be made to show, if it can, at least an equal measure of sense . . . . There can be no more urgent problem than their diagnosis."—George Dyson in *The New Music.*

### The Evolution of Our Major and Minor Scales from the Ecclesiastical Modes

Below we have the six authentic modes:

Ex.1

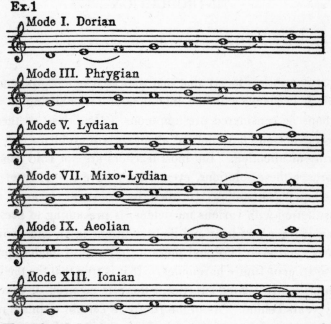

The Plagal Modes, II, IV, VI, VIII, X, XIV, are not here quoted, because they have the same finals, and order of intervals from the finals, as the authentic modes.

These modes of Greek origin form the basis of the music of the Polyphonic Period. Up to the end of the twelfth century the modes were utilized exactly as they stood except that, in harmonizing them, the diminished triad was not used with root in the bass unless the root was flattened; this was frequently done.

Ex.2

This process of alteration was called *Musica ficta*, artificial music, and was employed in various parts of a piece to

make the music more euphonious. As music was largely
dominated by the church, whose authorities looked askance
at these alterations, we find that the singers introduced these
accidentals at will, having no rules to limit this freedom.
Later, the accidentals were placed above the notes.

In the true close (*Clausula vera*) the *Canto fermo* pro-
gressed from the second degree to the final and the accom-
panying part proceeded from below the final up to it. In the
Ionian mode the close seemed more satisfactory than in some
of the other modes; so it became the rule that the penultimate
chord should present a major sixth or minor third for the true
close in all modes.

**Ex. 3**

Modes III, V, and XIII naturally fulfill this condition.

**Ex. 4**

*Musica ficta* is employed in Modes I, VII, and IX to fulfill
the above requirements.

In Mode v (Lydian), in order to avoid the false relation of the tritone, $b^\flat$ was introduced at the cadence point.

**Ex.5**

It became the custom, when more than two voices were employed, to use the major third in the final chord, so we find the following cadences:

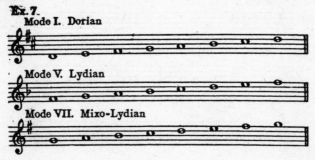

Notice that in Mode III the accidental in the penultimate chord is absent since the major sixth is acquired without it; so even in *Musica ficta* this mode retained more of its original feeling than some of the others.

When, employing the accidentals used in the cadences, we come to write the scales, we find them identical with the Ionian mode (Major mode), except in the case of the Phrygian mode. The Dorian sixth (*b*, major sixth) came to be used in the Aeolian mode (*f*♯), probably because of the augmented second between *f* and *g*♯. So one can see how the modes lost their identity.*† The two forms of the minor scales, by means of *Musica ficta* (applied to the seventh of the Dorian and Aeolian, respectively), were easily produced. "So the old rich modal system handed down to us by the Greeks was gradually reduced to only three scales—the major and two minor—which formed during more than three centuries the 'tonal loom' on which every melody was woven."— Alfredo Casella, *The Evolution of Music.*

This transformation was not accomplished in a short space of time. As a matter of fact, it was the development of several centuries. (Without *Musica ficta* the modes are notably dull and lifeless, the best modal writing employing both the pure modes and mixed forms of them.) The semitone at cadence points is responsible for this transformation. The introduction of the raised leading tone lends a virility to all our modern music, notwithstanding the abuse of this type of cadence. As might be expected, the tendency of the times is to return, somewhat, to the modal scales for fresh material. "That they might remain pure and distinct, the modes had to be rigid. Within their prescribed limits they were vehicles of a remarkable intimacy of expression. It was this that destroyed them. The most harmonically flexible of them in the end supplanted the others."—*The New Music,* by George Dyson.

---

*"The most humorous part of the story is that after centuries of gradual and continuous progress they ultimately completed a scale which they had known all along, but had rather looked down upon as an inferior specimen of its kind." —C. Hubert H. PARRY.

†For further explanation see Dr. Charles H. Kitson's *Evolution of Harmony.*

Now we have become so surfeited with music founded on the scales of the two modes, major and minor, that we are unable easily to understand or appreciate the music of periods before this development.    It is only in recent years that American musicians have become responsive to the quaint beauty of modal music.    It is doubtful whether anyone living to-day can have the same impression of, and regard for the music of the sixteenth century that musicians contemporary with it must have had.    How many listeners are able to tell, from hearing alone, in what mode a piece is written? There are a few such, however, and the composers who are so educated are the ones who are writing original music.

It is doubtless true that it is an impossibility to create an original melodic motive in our major mode.    This scale has been used so excessively by musicians, both learned and unlearned, that almost any melody conceived in it gives only the feeling of its being made up of trite components.    It is likely to be empty, void of freshness or originality, notwithstanding any complex harmony that may accompany it.

It is highly probable that artificial scales such as Busoni suggests in his *A New Aesthetic of Music* will be the solution of the matter.    No doubt the modal scales, when first suggested, gave the impression of being contrived by as deliberate a process as that by which Busoni has evolved his scales.*

Either a new series will be used or the scale lines will be obliterated.    Where chromatic progressions are constantly made use of, these lines are showing signs of disappearing.

The recent investigations in the quarter-tone and third-tone realms begin to indicate refreshing results, notwithstanding the complete revolutionizing of our musical system.†

After observing some of the close harmony shown in the following example (where the chords blend with surprising consistency notwithstanding their derivation from the upper harmonics), one is led to believe that the harmonic possibil-

*See footnote, Page 118.
†Investigate works in this line by Alois Haba, Prague.

ities of the quarter or third-tone system will sometime be practicable.

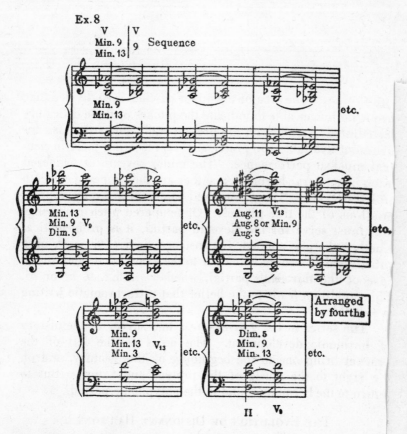

These chords employ the farther advanced of the overtones; others would make necessary fractional divisions, or ultrachromaticism. Scriabine's experiments, followed to their logical conclusion, would lead to a division of the semitone. His ideas actually belong to the ultrachromatic plan.

A study of the harmonic series convinces one that the evolution of the present semitonal harmonic system is nearing

completion.   The area of the upper partials is so divided that
one is no longer able to indicate the pitches of these delicately
distributed overtones on the present staff, nor is there an instrument available for practically representing them in general musical performance.   The minor seventh of tempered
pitch is not a true harmonic; neither are the tempered eleventh
and thirteenth.   These tempered intervals are only approx-
imations of the true pitches.   Of tempered pitch renderings
that must serve for the eleventh partial, it is problematical
whether the one notated, for instance, in Ex. 9, as $f^\sharp$, or a
substituted $f\text{※}$ would be nearer to the exact pitch; and, in the
case of the thirteenth partial, whether, in Ex. 9, $a^\flat$ or $a^\natural$.
This condition leads to the belief that ultrachromatic writing
is possible.

The series in Ex. 9 gives one a fine survey of the history
of harmonic development.   The notes on the left of the
bracket bring one to the beginning of this century, and on
the right to the music of the present and future.   But to
return to the harmony found in the polyphonic period.

### The Evolution of Dissonant Harmony Through the Suspension

The development of harmony from sixteenth-century
methods is an interesting process.   It is largely a metamor-
phosis involving a point of view, i.e., the elevation of the
unessential to the essential.

The foundation of sixteenth-century music was the interval.   On the accents the following consonances were used:

major and minor thirds, perfect fifths, and octaves from the
bass; the minor third and major or minor sixth from the bass;
the major third and major sixth from the bass.

**Ex. 10**

These are the only intervals that could occur on the ac-
cented part of the bar without *preparation*—that is, any tone
could be sustained beyond its natural limits to form a dissonance on the next accent.* These sustained notes were called
suspensions, and this was the general type of dissonance (as
a primary phenomenon) used in the sixteenth century.† This
method of writing yields the following dissonances, the pre-
cursors of our modern harmony: the seventh which resolves
to the sixth, the ninth to the octave, the fourth to the third,
and the second to the third if suspension is below. Here we
find the beginnings of the dissonances of the classic period.
Even the seventh of our common dominant seventh chord was
not an essential member of the chord, if the word chord may
be applied to dissonant combinations used during that period.

This process of suspending notes enabled the different
voices to maintain their rhythmic independence; and at the
same time the composers of that period were not unaware of
the emotional effect of the discords, and perhaps were cognizant of the possibility of employing them for a harmonic
and not a purely rhythmic purpose.

A few illustrations will suffice to show the methods employed. In Ex. 11, at (a), we find the seventh prepared by a
consonance at (b) and resolved at (c).‡ So we see that this

*Passing and embellishing notes not relevant here.
†Knud Jeppesen, in his book *The Style of Palestrina and the Dissonance*, recognizes three phases of the dissonance; first, dissonance as a secondary phenomenon (melodically induced, accidental dissonance); second, dissonance as a
primary phenomenon ("musical" dissonance in conscious, deliberately stressed
contrast to consonance); and third, dissonance employed as a means of poetical
expression.
‡The bass note in the second measure was considered an organ-point, the tenor
serving as bass, according to a convention of the period.

suspension is none other than the seventh of our modern dominant, skillfully handled. This is one of the first dissonances to have thrown off its shackles and is now used freely, so that

Ex. 11                                                        PALESTRINA

the unessential has become an essential.

Even the seventh in the bass was first used as a suspension. See Ex. 12, (a):

Ex. 12

Early writers had no thought of the seventh being in the bass, in such a passage as the foregoing, for such clarification of it was unknown at that time. It was analyzed as a suspension of the third.

The supertonic seventh chord has a similar origin. In Ex. 13 at (a) the bass is concordant with the *d* a sixth above

Ex. 13

and also with *c*, a perfect fifth, hence a possible combination at that time; but now we analyze it as the third of the supertonic seventh chord. The apparent passing-tone has become essential. The progression in its incipient stage was probably as shown in Ex. 13, (b).

All other sevenths may be similarly accounted for. Ex. 14.

Sevenths were suspensions, prepared and resolved, until, in the latter works of Palestrina a sequence of suspensions or seventh chords (if we apply the modern analysis) resulted.

**Ex.14**

It is natural to understand why such skill was exercised in the handling of these dissonances when we remember that this music was sung without the aid of instruments, a difficult feat for singers of any period.

It was discovered later that the seventh could agreeably be taken or approached from the fifth, so we find the English school using the seventh in this way:

**Ex.15**

Later we find all minor sevenths being taken without preparation: Ex. 15, (a), (b), and (c).

The introduction of instrumental music was an aid to the freer use of dissonance.

"Harmony, which was originally conceived in a purely horizontal sense, as resulting from the momentary contact of three or four superimposed melodies, by slow degrees reached a *vertical* conception, where the composer isolates such and such a chord from the polyphonic movement and treats it separately as an independent entity released from *polymelodic* tyranny and from the prejudice of *part-writing*, thus arriving even at the suppression, first of the preparation and later the resolution, of sounds originally classed as *discords*.

"A profound study of the history of harmony reveals, in fact, that nearly all of our most daring chords already existed long ago in old music in a latent state, but always in a poly-melodic form."—Alfredo Casella in *The Evolution of Music.*

### THE EVOLUTION OF THE HIGHER DISCORDS
### THROUGH THE SUSPENSION
### RECENT DEVELOPMENTS
### THE DOMINANT NINTHS, ELEVENTHS, AND THIRTEENTHS

The suspension of the octave (9 to 8) became the precursor of the chord member of a ninth. If a suspending note is strongly emphasized, or retained beyond its natural limits, it begins to assume an importance not otherwise accorded it, and the ear is led to accept it as a chord member. So we find the ninth delaying the octave becomes a true ninth. This is all the more apparent if the ninth chord resolves direct to another chord.

The prepared dissonance in Ex. 16, at (a), becomes an essential chord tone at (b). It is no longer necessary to hear the resolution of 9 to 8 as shown at (a), but to hear it as at (b) where 9 is a legitimate chord member.

The history of the evolution of the suspension seems to have developed this independence, for at the present time the suspensions over the third and fifth of the dominant may become the true eleventh and thirteenth of the dominant just as the suspension over the octave became the ninth.

Note in Ex. 17 how the notes suspending the third at (a) and the fifth at (c) become *bona fide* eleventh and thirteenth at (b) and (d) respectively, where chromatic harmony is employed.

It is essential that one should employ, chiefly, chromatic harmony to make these effective.

The instance at (a) in Ex. 18 analyzed by English theorists as a v 13th with 11th is not entirely convincing; it appears too much like a suspended or (without the ties) an appoggiatura chord.

If, however, it resolves to a chord on another root, it assumes all the characteristics of a chord of the eleventh and thirteenth. Ex. 18, (b) and (c).

With the dominant, if the note suspending the third is retained, the chord in certain positions assumes the intervals of a chord of the perfect fourth.   Ex. 19, (a).

So we find melodies moving along this line of fourths without any attempt at final resolution.   See Holst excerpt (Ex. 292) in Chapter xx.

In the music of the most advanced composers the suspension has practically disappeared, so perhaps it has served its day.

### HARMONIC EVOLUTION THROUGH THE APPOGGIATURA

Appoggiaturas were not a feature of the polyphonic period.   They have the same dissonant effect as the suspension, but, as is well known, are equivalent to unprepared suspensions.   It is natural that the appearance of appoggiaturas should have come later, in history, than the suspension, because they were an outgrowth of the suspension.

The freer treatment of dissonances could come only after a period of strict writing.   During the romantic period, then, we find the following methods employed:

The appoggiatura is approached by skip from below at (a), and at (b) by a skip from above.   If one has observed the

varied transformations of the suspensions, he will be curious
as to whether the appoggiatura has undergone the same meta-
morphoses.   This has actually happened in almost the same
manner as with suspensions.*   In the instances shown in
Ex. 21, we find that the ninth is taken as an appoggiatura and

retained as a ninth.   We have an interesting illustration in
Ex. 22 in which the $c^\sharp$ introduced as an appoggiatura in Ex. 20
is now a chord tone.

Other more dissonant chords may be developed in corresponding ways.   Ex. 23.   Musicians know the usual ultimate
movement of the soprano note at (a), so the composer fre-

*See **Ex. 135, a good example of appoggiatura chords.**

Ex. 24

quently tries some other solution, as is shown at (b), Ex. 24.*
Here we have the appoggiaturas sounding as chord tones. In
Debussy's *Children's Corner* we find the appoggiaturas sounding at the same time as the principal notes. Numerous examples may be quoted from modern composers. While the
single appoggiaturas are being turned into chord tones, there
is a more pronounced tendency to make chords wholly of
appoggiaturas (appoggiatura chords). If one secures chromatic appoggiaturas for each voice of the chord, the ear
readily accepts such dissonances.

This latter method has become possible only since the
introduction of chromatic harmony. The added-note theory
also has been a contributing factor.

Ex. 25

Numerous examples of the dominant may be secured in
this way, some of which may become by usage essential chord
forms. See Ex. 135.

In the following example the appoggiaturas are unresolved, thereby becoming legitimate chord tones, here the
ninth and thirteenth. Can they not be accepted as such without an intervening resolution? See Ex. 26 (a), and at (b)
their resolutions.

*Such chords have only a temporary significance.

## The Influence of the Chromatic Passing-Tone

### On Harmony

Chromatic passing-tones frequently become *bona fide* chord members. Ex. 27. The formations at (a) are passing and at (b) are regular chords.

The chord at (b) in the measure next to the last in the examples above is a dominant minor ninth with a raised fifth, a lowered fifth, and an augmented ninth.*

Here, at (a), is the unresolved appoggiatura, serving as a thirteenth.

*See Chapter XII.

Ex.28

The following also is of about the same type.   This is called

Ex.29

by some a free anticipation, and by others the thirteenth.

## THE NEAPOLITAN CHORD

The early form of the Neapolitan chord was probably from the Phrygian scale where it occupies a position a half step above the initial note, its resolution at that time being entirely different from its modern use.*   There is, however, another explanation for its origin.   The altered chords that are in common use were probably developed through chromatic passing-tones.   The Neapolitan chord was first used in minor; therefore it was a simple matter to develop it from the passing-tone as shown in Ex. 30, at (a) and at (b), by taking the latter as a chord member.

*The Neapolitan chord in the Phrygian mode could not resolve to the dominant-chord because that chord was a diminished one.

The false relation between the Neapolitan sixth and the dominant is allowed.

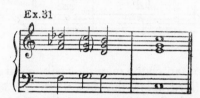

Elision of the tonic six-four is here illustrated.

The prevailing idea in recent years with regard to chords in general is that they may be used interchangeably between major and minor, so we find the use of the Neapolitan chord frequent in major.

We may expect the Neapolitan sixth to have become enlarged to an eighth, and even to seventh and ninth chords.* Ex. 128.

The Neapolitan triad with root in bass may be resolved best in two ways: first, to the dominant six-four-three; and second, to the dominant six-five.

*A seventh or ninth added to a Neapolitan triad would not cancel its Neapolitan implications.

Sometimes the root of the tonic six-four appears as a passing-tone and then it is virtually the seventh of a Neapolitan seventh.* The six-five inversion occasionally appears, but again as a passing seventh.

The Neapolitan chord may be easily enlarged by placing a diminished third below the root, as in Ex. 33 (b), so as to form a VII chord; then the process described in Chapter IX, i.e., *The Augmented Fourth Relationship*, begins to take on reasonableness, as also does Ex. 45.

## THE AUGMENTED SIXTH CHORDS

The augmented sixth chords may be accounted for on the same basis. Note the passing-tones in Ex. 34.

If we assume that these chords were first used in minor, the only alteration necessary is to raise the major sixth to an augmented sixth.

*In Brahms' *Requiem*, chorus, "How Lovely is Thy Dwelling Place."

Ex. 35

The origin of the v augmented 6-4-3 is even more simple: a passing-note taken as bass note in the second inversion of the dominant seventh.

Ex. 36

## THE INFLUENCE OF MODULATION ON HARMONY

The subject of modulation is one of vital importance in musical theory and practice, and it alone would require a complete treatise. In most ways this subject is well understood, having been covered in manifold ways by erudite theorists. Because of this, and because problems in other lines still await discussion, the author has decided to touch only lightly on the subject.

The process of modulation was first limited to occasional changes of key, mostly to the ones nearly related and was effectuated by means of the common triads, dominant sevenths, and diminished sevenths. Later, more startling modulations were employed through the deceptive resolutions of augmented and dominant seventh chords; even through the Neapolitan chord. Still later, the so-called common-tone modulation became current, being frequently employed by all composers, e.g., Wagner, in *Lohengrin* (Elsa's Dream). As in common-chord modulation, so now the common tone acts, but with greater facility, as a pivot upon which to adjust or rotate the key. If we hear, for example, the third in the soprano, it may become a root by assuming it to be such and treating it accordingly. Ex. 37. Passing-notes, appoggiaturas, suspensions, and even altered notes may all have their direction instantly changed and their resolution with their new harmonic implications readjusted accordingly, if one desires to make the necessary assumptions.

In recent years, chromatic music has become such a familiar product that the scope of tonality has been extended further than was formerly thought possible, including all half steps under the domain of one key, not as passing-notes but as legitimate chord members of altered chords, such as those shown in Ex. 46. Modulation increased outside of this tonality scheme, however, in scope and frequency until we have simultaneous chord groups comprising chords of different keys. This placing together of two or more tonal systems has brought diametrically opposed harmonic clusters into direct juxtaposition; but in music, as in art: "When red and green are juxtaposed, the red increases the saturation of the green and the green that of the red, so that both colors are heightened in brilliance."—J. Ward.

This brings harmony to the position where the vertical aspect of the chord group is no longer a consideration; its parts may contain all notes of a chromatic scale, for the persistent movement of two or more parts in some predetermined progression may at times demand such cacophonic combinations, if consistency is to be a consideration in its formation. See Ex. 38.

The subject of "atonality" is a mutable one. By some, atonal music is considered to be that without key center; by others music with uncertain key basis or changing tonality. Hugo Leichtentritt, a German authority, contends: "Atonality seems a convenient subterfuge for chaos and nonsense. Music as an art can dispense with tonality as little as architecture can disregard the straight line, the perpendicular, the center of gravity. 'Atonality' is only tonality in disguise, in a new and surprising variation which we must learn to understand and to interpret properly. The major and minor keys do not exhaust tonality." If however, we can create a semitonal melody without the ever-intruding diatonic entanglements and implications, a new atonal atmosphere may be established; at least it will be something different than that associated with diatonicism.

More and more demands have been made on the musical listener in recent years by this constant readjustment and re-alignment of our listening powers, so the harmonic problems of the present day are manifold.

Ex. 38 is an instance of two harmonic streams.

*J. & W. Chester, Ltd.

### Consecutive Fifths

The first consecutive fifths to be used acceptably in modern music were commonly called the Mozart fifths. These occur between the augmented 6-5 chord and the dominant. Ex. 39 (a).

Some theorists still contend that these are incorrect and prefer to resolve them to the tonic six-four chord as shown at (b).

The contention now by the best musicians is that consecutive fifths by chromatic progression are not so offensive as by diatonic movement.  Ex. 40.

Ex. 40

Dr. C. H. Kitson even intimates that they are really pleasant.  Perhaps this is the reason that so many composers have used consecutive dominant ninths, moving by semitones, where the fifths appear in parallel motion with the sevenths and ninths.  See Chapter II for further discussion.

If one desires the crude effect produced by fifths, he should not be condemned for writing them.  It all depends on the impression he wishes to convey.  The composer who wishes to be versatile must be able to write in a variety of ways.

Sir Charles Stanford has alleged (Proceedings of the Musical Association, 1922) that fifths "are as ugly now as they ever have been, as they ever will be, world without end . . . . because their ugliness most probably depends upon natural phenomena and not upon individual taste." This only shows with what seriousness musicians of the recent past regarded the use of fifths. It has been remarked that "new theories and laws do not necessarily disprove old ones, but explain certain discrepancies in them and penetrate more deeply into their underlying principles. To follow the new reasoning, we must rid ourselves of the prejudice behind the old, not because it is wrong, but because it is insufficient" (Bird, *Relativity and Gravitation*). This might be applied to musical laws.

Eugène Goosens suggests that fifths fell into disuse, being superseded by other progressions, "so that," in the words of Schönberg, "again the ear was prepared to find such combinations new and even surprising."

M. D. Calvocoressi in his book, *Musical Criticism*, says "The ear, as we know, is essentially susceptible to education; the average ear nowadays accepts without a qualm things that were intolerable a few decades ago. But with regard to any particular point, be it chromaticism, fifths, consecutive ninths, or the atonality and polyphony of to-day, certain ears need education and are modified by it. Others do not need it, still others remain unaffected by it. It is therefore safe to admit that the matter is, at least partly, one of natural physical disposition."

## Further Considerations

The ready acceptance of the method whereby the seventh chord appeared to resolve upwards, as employed during the sixteenth century, has been a difficult problem, but if one can regard it from the contrapuntal point of view it is not hard to comprehend. See Ex. 41.

Ex. 41

The *f* and *d* were passing-tones, and the *b* was an embellishment tone, all three accessory to one harmony. Here however, the unessential have become essential, and a chord of the dominant six-four-three has resulted. The resolution of the seventh as shown in Ex. 42 (a substituting resolution) is a modern device, but may have been derived from the above; it is now applied to all discords.

Ex. 42

The old modal system was quite unfitted for the artistic purposes of harmony, and that gradual blending and assimilation of the modes into a system of keys was a necessary preliminary to the development of true harmonic music of the modern kind. The sixteenth-century writers had no conception of the tonic and dominant as we now consider them, neither had they an understanding of modulation as now applied. Flats and sharps were not introduced to give the effect of a change of key, but to avoid awkward melodic intervals and at certain cadences to give a more satisfactory close, where the desire for a penultimate major chord (a harmonic consideration) was as prominent in their minds as the desire for a semitonal rise to a final tone (a melodic consideration).

The key feeling is much more definite than the modal, probably because the modal melody may begin and end on almost any note of the series, for in all melodic systems the notes are more on an equality. Their functions are not decisively fixed. "The modern European scheme of art [before the advent of the present tendencies] rests upon a systematization of the scale, which recognizes certain notes as being final, and all other notes as having relative degrees of importance, . . . . it is purely the result of harmonic development."—*Evolution of the Art of Music*, by C. Hubert H. Parry.

After more than two centuries of supremacy of the diatonic outlook, the limitations of the diatonic scales are becoming more pressingly realized than ever before. "Impurity of mode in the form of a gradually increasing proportionate importance assigned to chromatic elements is one of the entering wedges in modern music which has brought about a weakening of tonal concentration."—*Rise and Decline of Tonality*, by George Dickinson, Proceedings of the M.T.N.A., 1922. The use of the whole-tone scale has also had its influence in vitiating the tonal center; its effect has been antitonal, but to quote further from George Dickinson, in regard to the returning influence of medieval modes which now act reciprocally on diatonic tonality: "In the same fashion in which their dominance in the sixteenth century restrained the persuasion of tonality, their present influence is in the nature of an undermining of tonal logic . . . . There has been a constructive purpose involved however: the veiled and unresponsive quality of music which exploits the non-tonal modes is a genuine expressive resource, just as it was in the sixteenth-century polyphony."

One harmonic progression, very suggestive of modal procedure, may be emphasized in connection with a resolution in modal harmony, the so-called retrogressive progression, i.e., the dominant resolving to subdominant, or the supertonic to the tonic, etc. In the Dorian mode a progression of this type would give the result shown at (a) in Ex. 43, and the modern form in the key of *C* might be as shown in Ex. 43 (b)

The following unusual resolution of the seventh in the bass was probably evolved in this way, according to C. H. Kitson.

All problems previously mentioned are now becoming understood. Even Wagner's complex harmonies which are founded on diatonic tonality, even if they are complexly chromatic, have been more or less rationalized by theorists. If one can trace the continuously modulatory methods of this great composer, his music becomes much simplified. Musicians are rare to-day who cannot follow his complex scores with complete satisfaction, but with the more recent composers this is almost impossible.* So we are led to the modern harmonic problems.

*"During the last thirty years the externals of creative Musical Art have changed; in a sense, almost beyond recognition." From an article before the Music Teachers National Association, 1926, on "Contemporary European Music," by Eugène Goossens.

CHAPTER I

## MODERN HARMONIC PROBLEMS

Only a year or two since, an article* was written by
Emerson Whithorne suggesting that musical production had
come to the end of the road, and to many this has seemed to
be its present status. But if one is in touch with the different
movements, he will discover that there are many directions
in which music is turning, which augurs well for the future.
Probably the outstanding indication of progress is the break-
ing down of tonality restrictions, or the enlarging of the
domain which one given key may encompass.

Much theory teaching does not take into consideration
that there are numerous altered chords surrounding a given
tonality which may be used without giving the impression of
a modulation. That there are indications of such usage, thus
bringing the chromatic notes within the diatonic realm, is
indicated in a paper read by George W. Gow before the
M. T. N. A., 1926. Speaking of the theory of music during
the past fifty years: "No one made the observation that many
a transient modulation, so called, is none at all in effect, since
the objective of the chromatic ripple, when reached, remains
securely in its status in the original key. Now we have become aware that the conception of key far oversteps the limits
of the diatonic, and that outside of key in its mildest interpre-
tation there exists still a fascinating tone region only partly
explored."

Every possible triad, seventh, and even ninth chord, may
be brought into touch with any given tonic without there being

*Modern Music, Nov., 1926, "Where Do We Go From Here?"

29

a change of key. Take the complex and distinctive harmony shown in Ex. 45 for example:

This can be easily associated with the key of *C major* without any thought of modulation. Also the major triads shown in Ex. 46 may be a part of the key of *C major*.

César Franck uses in his *Beatitudes* a progression utilizing the relationship between the *C* and *E♭* triads. The use of apparently foreign harmony brings a large contribution to the effectiveness of modern composition.

## THE ANCIENTISTS

There are a few musical producers who see much promise in a revival of modal scales. Now that the present major and minor scales are becoming effete by constant usage, this desire for a return to former methods to secure revitalizing material is hopefully prophetic. One cannot expect to regain the purity of their utilization by the musicians who developed them, but the new vitality of result one secures from them after close association with the classical key systems is impressive. If one observes the following scales, transposed to show them in their relation to scales of the classic key system, one is more convinced of their efficacy in the production of a newer music.

Ex. 47

A number of recent composers have written music with a degree of modal atmosphere together with a type of harmony suggestive of recent harmonic developments. If one writes music of this kind he should avoid the dominant seventh of the classic period, but the secondary sevenths do not detract from the feeling of sublimity surrounding the old music.

Some one has said, "The ancient modes combine a solemnity and a grandeur with the most tender and fervent devotion. Their minor cadences give not so much the impression of sadness as of great solemnity and awe; their major tendencies not so much the impression of merriment as of a tender and ardent devotion."

Influences of this sort upon modern musical thinking would not be at all detrimental.

## Linear Counterpoint

Another type of music of which Schönberg and Stravinsky seem to be leaders is that of "linear counterpoint." This involves counterpoint of the most dissonant kind without regard for the consonances thought necessary in the old music. It takes into account the independent movement of diverse melodic streams involving unorthodox counterpoint of the more drastic type.

## Polytonalists

Another group applies its talents to the working out of polytonal music which is motivated by the simultaneous progression of two or even more tonal systems. These, beside necessitating the proper formation of the separate streams, also demand the adjustment of these so that they may blend agreeably.

## Atonalists

The atonal writers endeavor to overthrow the autocracy of a key center, or at least leave it so uncertain by constant key shifting that no definite tonality is discernable.

## The Fractional Tone Music

Others are applying their efforts to the development of the "ultrachromatic" idea. Busoni conceived the idea of thirds of tones, and Haba of Prague has written a quarter-tone quartet. A quarter-tone clarinet and a piano with these additions have been constructed. Julian Carillo, the Mexican composer, presented at the New York concerts of the League of Composers, and in Philadelphia with the Philadelphia Symphony Orchestra, some of this fractional tone music. A. Eaglefield Hull contended that new harmonic material to the extent of 253 three-note chords and more are possible with the ultrachromatic key system.*

## The Hurlyburlists

Irving Weil in an article in *Modern Music* believes that the noisemakers (the hurlyburlists) are pioneers in a most stimulating movement because they are doing something which may be more valid than most of us think, and may be

*See article by A. Eaglefield Hull in *Musical Digest*, winter of 1928, "Will Quarter-Tones Come?"

at the beginning of what the music of the future will be. The chief representatives of this school are Edgar Varèse and George Antheil. Their efforts are concentrated on the development of rhythm with all its intricate complexities contrasted to the utmost degree. They have combined dissonances in a more drastic way than Stravinsky has in his *Sacre du Printemps*. Together with this highly complex rhythmical fabric Varèse employs very dissonant harmony, a harmony of tone qualities, upon which he places much stress. In order to give his musical texture the proper dynamic force, he puts much emphasis on percussion instruments, proportionately more than any other composer has done.

So we find many harmonic problems for the theorist to consider, but it is becoming more necessary to take into consideration tone color in order to explain intricate harmonies. Some of these problems will be discussed in this book.

If one will attempt to analyze an excerpt from *Pacific 231*, by Honegger, as an example of present-day music, he will not question the complexity of the task before him.

The effect of tone color, in connection with its mollifying influence on dissonant harmony (and which has become such an important issue in present-day composition, involving the possible formations of chord groups in succession, so complex that no sort of reasonable analysis can be propounded), has led the theorists to believe that wrestling with the problem of analysis of the chord group, and even that of resolution, is no longer necessary.

This is particularly true of orchestral music, where the sheer harmonic beauty of the most dissonant group, with colorful orchestration, gives one no feeling of a need of resolution as it did in the past.

Dissonances of the older type gave one the feeling of restlessness, a desire to move forward to consonance; they were endured because of the expected relief and consequent satisfaction. Now that this feeling of completeness is secured with each succeeding chord, the urge is not so compelling.

\* Ex. 48   Pacific 231. Mouvement symphonique

A. HONEGGER

\* Edition Maurice Senart.

## Chapter II

# THE RESOLUTION OF SEVENTHS AND NINTHS

If one is inclined to be somewhat conservative about resolutions of sevenths, a satisfactory method that meets with general approval may be employed in the following manner: sevenths may be resolved upward, provided the bass takes the note of resolution. This is most admirably brought out in A. E. Heacox's harmony books. See Ex. 49.

Ex. 49

Sevenths and ninths may also be resolved upward, using them impressionistically, if one is leading his chords in parallel motion and degreewise. See Ex. 50.

Ex 50  Madame Butterfly  G. PUCCINI

*G. Ricordi and Co.

To many it will be a decided surprise to know that Chopin wrote passages of consecutive seventh chords in parallel motion in his *Twenty-first Mazurka.*

Ex. 51   Mazurka, Op. 30, № 4
*Tempo di Mazurka*                                          CHOPIN

Dr. George Dyson, in his book *The New Music,* calls this progression the "side-slip" (normally chords move with a skip relationship of roots—for instance, upward or downward by a fifth or fourth).   Ninths are much used in this way, Debussy perhaps being the originator of such methods.   In his *Pelléas and Mélisande* we find the following:

*Ex. 52   Pelléas and Mélisande                            DEBUSSY

* A. Durand & Fils.

This is known as the impressionistic method. The idea involved in a system of this kind is that if one chord creates a favorable impression, a series of chords of the same kind will increase this favorable condition.

"These chords thus become points of rest, not so much because their normal inferences are discounted as because they cease to have any in such a context." *The New Music,* by George Dyson.

These dominant sevenths and ninths may be alterations of the common secondary seventh and ninth chords of any given key (see Chapter x, where they are treated more fully), or they may be borrowed dominants of different keys, the key feeling being temporarily abandoned, and resumed after the final dominant. If these chords are used in the impressionistic manner, parallel fifths result. The latter are perfectly agreeable in such an environment. See Ex. 54.

This continuous movement of sevenths and ninths, constantly shifting,* tends to loosen the original key feeling because normally we expect the dominant to satisfy our desire for finality by progressing to a tonic. This constant changing of key feeling until no key is apparent has given rise to the term "atonalism." See footnote on page 93.

With regard to parallel fifths, it is a most desirable arrangement if the sevenths move with the fifths, especially in the lower parts. The fifths are not disagreeable; neither are the sevenths, with such leading.

Ex. 53

"Theorists must now recognize that consecutive fifths[†] may often be excellent in effect, and that consecutive discords may be quite satisfactory. It cannot be too strongly empha-

*The impressionistic method explains such unusual resolutions.
†See Page 24.

sized that laws of progression which referred to harmony which was mainly diatonic must be considerably modified when the whole gamut of chromatic resource is utilized."— *The Evolution of Harmony*, Dr. C. H. Kitson, Royal College of Music, London.

It must be remembered that harmony as presented in this book is mainly for instrumental use. A composer in writing at the present time seldom requires his chorus to follow the complete harmony, as the orchestra takes that, and the chorus follows some simple melodic line. It is a very easy task for instruments to play where voices would be entirely at sea. So why should the voice parts be required to include all the essential harmonic strands?

To return to the models shown in Ex. 53, one can add the following parts:

Ex. 54

A number of sevenths may be thought of melodically; in that case their harshness is much reduced and their resolution may be somewhat free. The seventh may move ornamentally a third higher and return one degree.

Ex. 55

The genesis of this may have been as follows:

Ex. 56

Other chords may be similarly used.

Ex 57

These fifths are another example of correct leading, notwithstanding their visual prominence, because their audibility is negligible.

More and more license has become common both in the preparation and in the resolution of dissonances; all great composers took advantage of this freer treatment if they deemed it advisable. The freedom of resolution came when the expected resolution was ignored and the unexpected was advanced as a happy solution. This fondness for dissonance at the time of resolution is a device that has a lure for the modern writer: not only one dissonant chord may appear, isolated from other dissonant chords, but sometimes a con-

tinuous stream of such.    This then becomes a color effect of
dissonance, the emphasis being placed on the color mass
rather than on the resolving tendency of these chord com-
plexes; indeed, these dissonances are sometimes not analyzable along the old lines.

In diatonic writing, this feeling for resolution and what
it should be has been a perception which all apparently have
possessed, this being one of the greatest arguments for the
primordial superiority of diatonic tonality.    Whether this
has been entirely a matter of training and education, time will
tell.    Because of this perception of the expected resolution
of a chord, the unexpected gains its freshness.    These dissonant chords, chosen for their pungent flavor, are satisfying in
themselves, all other considerations being secondary.    This
should account for some of the harmonic effulgence of the
products of latter-day composers, whose sole aim may be, at
times, to give their music a luster heretofore unknown.

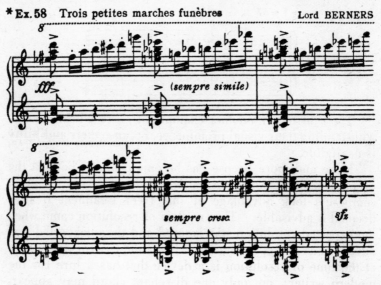

*Ex. 58    Trois petites marches funèbres                    Lord BERNERS

*J. & W. Chester, Ltd.

## CHAPTER III

# THE MODAL DOMINANT

## (MODERN APPLICATION)

One of the great harmonic losses in the transition from modal music to modern scales was the almost complete abandonment of the minor dominant. In modern instrumental music one can seldom find such, and yet it imparts a nobly serene atmosphere.

In Ravel's *Sonatine*, in the second part, he uses this cadence:

\* Ex. 59  Sonatine
Mouvement de Menuet                    MAURICE RAVEL

It is true that the early theorists had no such conception of chords as we now have, but in our modern thought the feeling here is of dominant with lowered third.

It is only within recent years, since we have found our two scales (major and minor) worn threadbare, that much emphasis is being laid on a return to old modal scales. It is probable that this will not be consummated in its entirety, because there is a virility and optimism about the Ionian scale that is not found in any other. But any of the important traits of the old scales that can be transplanted and included in our modern technic, whether it be melodic or harmonic,

\*Durand & Fils.

should be readily accepted.   If we recall the final measures
of Grieg's *Piano Concerto*, in which he employs the minor
dominant with major ninth and minor seventh, we will surely
be convinced of its value.

The minor dominant has been emphasized so long in the

Ex. 60

serious music of the church that the assumption has been that
it cannot be of importance elsewhere.

*Ex. 61   Indian Legend (For Organ)          Later          H. A. M.

These old cadences should not be discarded, for a certain
quaintness would be lost if one should resort to using the half
step.   A frequent use of the lowered leading tone in minor
will help to maintain this atmosphere, whereas the half step
imparts a certain sensuousness.

It is this old modal whole step that lends allurement to
the collecting of native folk-songs.   The presence of this
lowered leading tone inevitably suggests antiquity.

*Novello & Co.

Ex 62    In der Heimath, Op. 43, № 3

GRIEG

In the fragment of an Indian folk-song quoted in Ex. 61,
it will be noticed that the *b* in the second measure is a whole
step from the keynote *c sharp* in the next measure.   Upon
repetition of this phrase later in the piece the modern half
step *b sharp* is employed to give variety.   The quaintness of
many folk-songs has been destroyed by this raised leading
tone, and the restoration of their true character is frequently
possible by reintroducing the whole step.*   We find in Ex. 62
another cadence by Grieg quite similar to the former, that is,
he makes use of the minor dominant and major ninth.

A more recent use of this minor dominant will be found
in Leo Sowerby's arrangement of *Money Musk*.   See Ex. 63,
(a).   Later he harmonizes the same phrase in the way shown
at (b), Ex. 63.   Here the harmony suggests the process of
construction in fourths, or, as some would say, the dominant
eleventh.

Ex. 63   Money Musk

(b)

LEO SOWERBY

*See Helen Hopekirk's rearrangement of Scotch folk-songs.
†C. C. Birchard & Co.

Another illustration of a modal dominant is given in Ex. 64.

Ex. 64

Indian Theme

## Chapter IV

# ALTERED FORMS OF THE AUGMENTED
# SIXTH CHORDS

## (Alterations and Additions)

The most necessary member of an augmented sixth chord is of course the augmented sixth. This is usually accompanied by an augmented fourth or perfect fifth (doubly augmented fourth) and regularly by a major third. New variations of these appear now and then, i.e.:

Augmented sixth with minor third instead of major.

Augmented fifth instead of perfect fifth.

The addition of a doubly augmented octave to the chord. Major third, augmented fourth, augmented fifth, augmented sixth, doubly augmented octave.

The augmented third and major third (a diminished octave apart) to the $6^+$ chord.

### The Augmented Sixth with Minor Third

In Edward Elgar's *Caractacus* he employs this more rarely used chord.

*Ex. 65    Caractacus

E. ELGAR

*Novello & Co.

While it might be built on other bass notes than the fourth degree of the scale, it has been used in that location, which, for the present, we might assume to be the best one for it. Its preparation might be secured in the following ways:

Ex. 66

II₆

One will recall a passage in *Ase's Tod*, by Grieg, in connection with this. When more use is made of chromatic harmony, this chord will find its place.

## The Doubly Augmented Octave Added to the Augmented Chord

A growing desire for an enlarged augmented 6-5 and 6-4-3 chord is in evidence. The audible effect of the augmented 6-5 is the same as that of a dominant seventh; it is the resolution that determines the nature of the chord. Any dominant ninth may be converted into some kind of an augmented chord. By writing the ninth as a doubly augmented octave from the bass and resolving it upward to a tonic 6-4-3 in major keys, an interesting progression ensues. See Ex. 67.

Ex. 67

6+                                                    etc.

## The Augmented Fifth in Connection with
## Augmented Chords

If one has serious scruples concerning the use of the consecutive fifths in the resolution of the augmented chord, they may easily be avoided by substituting an augmented fifth for the perfect fifth or the doubly augmented fourth.* See Ex. 68. Indeed with the inclusion of the augmented fifth, we are in part using whole-tone harmony described in Chapter xiv.

Ex. 68

## Doubly Augmented Octave and Augmented Fifth
## Added to Six-Four-Three Chord

When we use chords with augmented intervals they are suggestive of whole-tone chords. As the intervals of a whole-tone scale from the keynote are major second (doubly augmented octave), major third, augmented fourth, augmented fifth, and augmented sixth, this last chord of six notes includes that complete scale in its make-up just as does the whole-tone dominant ninth with lowered and raised fifth. See Chapter xiv.

This chord can rightfully be called the whole-tone augmented chord. We here emphasize the fact that the whole-tone harmonies are the most important part of the whole-tone idea.

In Ex. 69 (a) we find the augmented chord resolving to a

*See first few measures of Scriabine's *Le Poème de L'Extase.*

tonic 6-4-3 with the major seventh present, a rather novel resolution, but the tonic 6-4 feeling is still there. In Ex. 69 (b) it resolves directly to the dominant seventh; at (c) the bass note is on the fourth degree of the scale, and the doubly augmented octave is written as a major second; the effect is plagal.

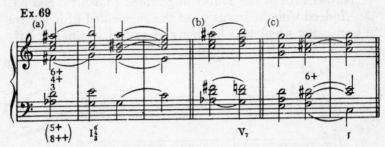

## THE AUGMENTED SIXTH WITH THE AUGMENTED THIRD

Other new augmented chords built on the same bass note, with augmented third above the bass note, may be used. They have been written but never analyzed. Some are called embellishing chords, others passing chords; if, however, they are located and labeled, perhaps they can be used in a rational way instead of by accident.

Use from the bass note, in the order indicated: augmented third, augmented sixth, and major third. In Ex. 70 we find the preparation and resolution of this chord.

Notice that the major third and augmented third are a diminished octave apart.

Ex. 70

## OTHER ALTERED FORMS
### MORE RARE COMBINATIONS

A number of other chords that do not contain the augmented sixth might also be classified here.  See Ex. 71.

**Ex. 71**

## THE DIMINISHED OCTAVE

A growing tendency among composers is to use the diminished octave in chords.  We have the same audible effect in the major seventh, but the peculiar voice leading in the case of each of these intervals makes it imperative that they should be written differently.

The desire for intensified expression is one of the impelling motives in the construction of chords employing the diminished octave, and piquancy is greatly emphasized in this way.

**Ex. 72**

A certain principle with regard to these chords and others may be advanced as almost axiomatic:—*If all voices in a chord move by half steps almost any combination of dissonances may be used, provided the voices are well dispersed.* Indeed the chord to which this dissonant chord resolves may likewise be somewhat dissonant; at least, the preparation of sevenths, ninths, and thirteenths is nicely secured in this way. The dissonant nature of any one of the chords is easily accepted by the ear because of this chromatic resolution. With these chromatic notes may be included one voice that remains stationary, which may act as an organ-point.

The following example may now be examined with these observations in mind. Other processes of this kind can be imagined.

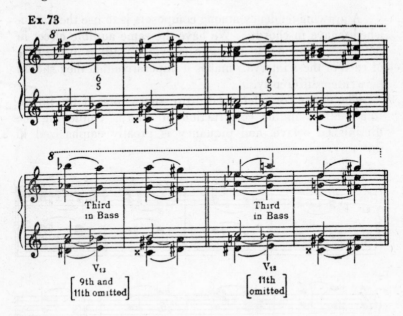

## CHAPTER V

# TRIADS WITH ADDED NOTES

The heretofore prevalent idea that only the tonic *triad* can represent the tonic feeling is now somewhat revised. *Most of the diatonic notes may be added to the tonic chord, probably (in the order of preference), sixth, ninth (or second), and seventh, and a feeling of finality is retained so long as the fundamental triad is predominantly in evidence.* The added sixth was applied first, perhaps, to the tonic triad. See Ex. 45. This was brought about in the following way:

The suspensions or appoggiaturas (see Ex. 74), were first resolved and later were retained as a part of the chord, no resolution taking place.

**Ex. 74**

Resolved Appoggiatura          Appoggiatura sounded with
the Principal Note

The ninth or second was added in much the same way. Lenormand tells us that Pere Sabbatini (1739-1809), a noted Italian theorist and composer, a pupil of Martini, published a treatise on chords, which included the addition of the ninth (or second) to the tonic. So this method is not as recent as many of us have assumed it to be.

But additions are no longer suggestive of being passing-notes or appoggiaturas. They are freely used, sometimes in an exaggerated manner with the inclusion of more notes than good judgment would warrant. The added sixth might be attached to practically any triad, provided the fifth and sixth are a major second apart.

In case of the dominant, the sixth is sometimes substituted for the fifth,* and frequently analyzed as the thirteenth. The tonic added sixth chord may have been suggested by an inclination to include members of the pentatonic scale in its make-up (see footnote on page 188). There seems to be a growing desire to combine all the notes of such a scale to make a chord. See Chapter XX.

By far the most striking innovation in added notes is the addition of a major seventh to the tonic (in major). Ex. 75, final chord.

Ex. 75    Slow Movement, Piano Sonata                    H. A. M.

Of course great care should be exercised in approaching it—a process that requires good musicianship.†

The added-note theory, in reality, brings a suggestion of the employment of two harmonies at the same time, and perhaps the notion of polytonality or polyharmony had its beginnings here. For example, when we use the added notes in Ex. 76 (a), (b), and (c), we are suggesting (a) the submediant triad; by the added seventh (b), the mediant; and by the added second and seventh (c), the dominant chord.

---

*See "Cumulative Harmony."—WILLIAM J. McCoy.
†Note in Ex. 75 where the penultimate chord employs the augmented ninth together with the raised fifth, resolving to the tonic chord with added seventh; this is one of the newer devices made possible through the use of chromatic harmony. See Ex. 135.

Note in Ex. 76 (d), (e), and (f), a few Scriabine cadences, made possible by "notes added to tonic," together with unique alterations of the dominant in its higher form.

If we once accept these final additions as agreeable concords,* a wonderful realm of enjoyment is unfolded, for the approach chord, i.e., dominant in all its various forms (e.g., the whole-tone chords and possible new additions to these), may be sounded with the tonic to enhance its beauty. See Chapter XII. The paramount reason for these additions, which, after all, justifies them, is the desire for less obvious harmony.

*The appearance of a common triad in connection with the continuous flow of a complex harmony would seem irrelevant; so by the taking on of other additions which do not obliterate the triad entirely, the uninterrupted succession of one type of harmony is gained.*

---

*The dominant seventh chord is now considered an agreeable concord. even though technically a discord.

## CHAPTER VI

## PARALLEL MOVEMENTS OF CHORDS
### (IMPRESSIONISTIC METHODS)

In the past, the parallel movement of chords was a rarity. If such a parallelism occurred, it was necessary to explain the exact reason. In the following example it was justified on the ground that the bass note *g* at (b) was really the same bass note as at (a):

Ex. 77

therefore the voices did not move in the same direction. Later it was found that there was no ill effect if the voices moved in the same direction to a diminished seventh chord. See Ex. 78 (Still another allowable instance was parallel movement from the tonic chord to the supertonic with the third in bass).

Ex. 78

Dim.
Chord

Later, Liszt, in his *Les Préludes* uses consecutive diminished seventh chords in parallel motion. This was perhaps the first impressionistic effect employing dissonant chords.

54

At the present time this parallelism has extended to many other combinations. In Wagner's *Siegfried* we find parallel movement of augmented triads; later, in Debussy's music we find parallel dominant seventh and dominant ninth in root position which had been suggested by Chopin and Liszt. Later we find inversions of the dominant chords in parallel motion and, again, secondary sevenths similarly used. See excerpt from F. H. Cowen's *The Veil* (Ex. 79).

\*Ex.79   Oratorio, The Veil
*Poco allegretto ma tranquillo*                           F. H. COWEN

[Consecutive six-four-three]

These are employed in a diatonic way, making use of the signature; they are also worked out chromatically. If one wishes to see the variety of ways in which parallel motion may be used, let him turn to Cyril Scott's works where he can find almost every known harmonic device. This composer uses chords in all inversions in parallel motion, ascending and descending.

An understanding of this method is an aid to the proper comprehension of harmony that would otherwise seem complex. Note, in Ex. 80 and 81, two chords used in this newer way. The first is a secondary seventh chord with the fifth lowered:

Ex.80

\*Novello & Co.

**Ex. 81** shows a chord which might be analyzed as a dominant ninth with seventh and fifth omitted and with thirteenth added. Here the fourths are present.

Ex. 81

Progressions of this type are not of the classic technic; they do not conform to the old ways. Even fifths used in parallel motion become as alluring as only thirds or sixths were at one time:

Ex. 82

After a certain amount of parallel movement one begins to desire contrary motion again, perhaps in one voice, so we find such passages as in Cyril Scott's Piano Sonata, Ex. 83.

\* **Ex. 83** Piano Sonata                    CYRIL SCOTT, Op.66

\*Elkin & Co., Ltd.

This leads on to the possibility of parallel movement within groups of harmonic voices, which *groups* are in contrary motion—a plan which has been very successfully applied to augmented chords.   See Ex. 160, Chapter XIV, where we find an exact mirroring.

Schönberg in his *Five Orchestral Pieces* employs three trumpets ascending with these augmented triads, and in contrary motion three trombones with minor triads; here also we find chromatic progression in each group of parts.   See Ex. 84.

Ex. 84   Five Orchestral Pieces, Op. 16   ARNOLD SCHÖNBERG

This leads on to polytonality, discussed in a later chapter. Many new chords have developed in this way, especially where the parts move slowly, e.g.:

Ex. 85

*Edition Peters.

## Chapter VII

# THE DOMINANT ELEVENTH AND THIRTEENTH

Very little is known of dominant elevenths and thirteenths in our American systems of teaching. The English and French are the ones who make use of analytical processes that recognize these chords, the former sometimes to an exaggerated degree (See Ex. 87, and comments on it).

The analyzing of music before Wagner will not require any knowledge of these chords; it is now, however, essential in order to grasp some of the modern methods.

The contention has been made that the dominant seventh differs from the higher discords in that the note of resolution requires a chord with another root. Until recent years this has not been true of the ninth, eleventh, and thirteenth; these have been resolved largely to the dominant seventh with the same bass note, therefore taking the form of suspensions and appoggiaturas; but now the unessential dissonances may become, and have become, the essential.

Since Wagner's time, the ninth has assumed such importance that the ninth chord may resolve directly to the tonic chord. With the introduction of chromatic harmony one is enabled to resolve the elevenths and thirteenths to chords with another root, thereby making use of these rarer dissonances to more varied advantage.

Ex. 86

This method has its real value and can be acquired easily by the student. The only wonder is that these higher discords have not been used more frequently (See Ex. 8).

The exact time and place when and where a combination of notes becomes a chord and not a *group* of suspensions and appoggiaturas, has been a subject of much discussion. It is largely a matter of the development of elision in our listening. Certain implied chords whose statement comes to be superfluous in progressions are no longer desired by the advanced composer, and he reveals to us newer methods.

These innovations are not always grasped at once by the general musical public. To a certain extent, seemingly satisfactory progressions are thus discarded for more doubtful ways, but the decided gain, if the process is reasonable, is soon apparent to the true musician.

Ex. 87

The author admits that numerous thirteenths can be analyzed as appoggiaturas; e.g., one English theory book calls the *e* in the following example a thirteenth:

Such reasoning is entirely inadequate. If the ninth, eleventh, or thirteenth resolves to the dominant seventh chord before the next chord appears, these dissonances should be called appoggiaturas, suspensions, or retardations, depending on the preceding harmony (See Ex. 88).

Ex 88
Two Chords     Appoggiatura

$V_{13}$   $V_9$        $V_7$        $V_9$

When our musical perception becomes so habituated to a certain resolution that we no longer require it, but preferably desire the immediate moving forward to another chord, thus eliminating the unnecessary step, then the first chord becomes a definite entity, and new harmony is born.    Textbook theorists can safely include such chords.    One is no longer required to complete the resolution in his auditory processes, this being merely the analytical aspect in connection with the evolution of harmony.    If one insists on such resolutions in listening, he is robbing himself of much of the real pleasure that music furnishes.

### The Dominant Eleventh

It will be obvious at once that if the eleventh is to be used, at least one of the other members of the chord will have to be omitted.

The eleventh (here *c*) is too harsh against the third (*b*) an octave below.    If the third is omitted, the effect is fairly satisfactory.

Numerous illustrations can be cited where these elevenths do assume a definite chord entity, notwithstanding the opposition of some theorists.    With the ever-increasing inclusion of dissonant harmonies as satisfying chords, it would appear that the following quotations (Ex. 90) will establish such chords as of separate and distinct classifications.

* Ex.90 (a) Pelléas et Mélisande                    DEBUSSY

*Durand & Fils.

Ex. 90 (b) Pelléas et Mélisande — DEBUSSY

VI₉   V₁₁   VI₉

## THE AUGMENTED ELEVENTH CHORD

The most agreeable form that the eleventh can take, in a chord of the eleventh or a chord of the thirteenth, occurs when it is altered to an augmented interval. This necessitates omitting the fifth. The chord now resembles the whole-tone dominant described in Chapter XIV. Ex. 91 show a satisfying treatment of this chord in parallel motion.

Ex 91

The augmented eleventh chord is suggested by notes in the harmonic series (Ex. 9), among the members of which are partials approximating the whole-tone scale. Scriabine's reasons for using this chord are therefore well founded. He frequently substitutes this interval for the fifth, but in *Prometheus* it is retained. In Scriabine's Piano Sonata, two measures of which are quoted in Ex. 92, a very precise method of this composer is shown. The augmented eleventh is in the bass.

Ex. 92   Piano Sonata, Op. 66, № 8                    SCRIABINE

If one employs the minor thirteenth and augmented eleventh of the major dominant with the fifth omitted, he secures one of the further developments of the whole-tone dominant described in Chapter XIV. In Ex. 114, measure three, this same augmented eleventh becomes enharmonically a $d^b$ and a new dominant is formed thereon.

Much depends on the handling of the fifth of the dominant and the half-steps immediately contiguous thereto. Nothing disrupts a key more effectually than to interfere with this interval. The third leads by half-step to a definite tonic, whereas the raised fifth produces an augmented triad, a chord which is ambiguous; and if lowered, it brings forward the fourth degree of the whole-tone scale, and that, in combination with the raised fifth, applied to the dominant ninth chord extends this series through the enharmonic of the augmented eleventh, and further enables it to point to harmonic connections outside of the diatonic realm. In other words, the fact that this raised and lowered fifth may be augmented eleventh and minor thirteenth of the dominant gives the altered fifth an elasticity and vagueness, advantage of which is often taken.

## The Dominant Thirteenth

The thirteenth is a much more desirable dissonance than the eleventh, although the two are much used together. It is essential again that intervals of the chord should be omitted to make it at all agreeable. The third and fifth are usually the ones omitted.

Perhaps the most natural use of a thirteenth on record is to be found in *Pelléas and Mélisande* by Debussy:

\*Ex. 93   Pelléas et Mélisande      DEBUSSY

This excerpt from Eugène Goossens' *Nature Poem,* Op. 25, No. 3, shows the use of the dominant thirteenth with the fifth in bass. Here the chord is used consecutively in parallel motion:

Ex. 94   Nature Poem, № 3      EUGENE GOOSSENS

For a thorough understanding of Scriabine's music, it is essential that the chords of the eleventh and thirteenth should be recognized.

In Ex. 95 are shown the various means this composer employs in constructing these chords. He places the augmented eleventh low in the chord, the thirteenth next to the top, as at (a). At (b) he uses the minor thirteenth with natural eleventh, and at (c) he uses both the augmented eleventh and minor ninth.

\*A. Durand & Fils.

By the inclusion of the eleventh and thirteenth we are enabled to build chords by fourths instead of thirds. See Chapter XIX for a fuller explanation of such methods.

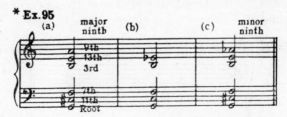

One great advantage in recognizing the eleventh and thirteenth as legitimate chord intervals is that one is thereby enabled to skip freely from such chord members in a similar way as from others, so we find Scriabine using the following progression:

He moves independently from the *a*, the augmented eleventh in the first measure, and again from *c*, the thirteenth in the second measure. See also the excerpt from his Étude, Ex. 114.

Our American theorists have had difficulty in properly classifying some melodic notes. They have called them "free tones." If we accept the eleventh and thirteenth as chord tones, the difficulty is eliminated in the only kinds of situations in which it can arise.

*The chord at (a) in Ex. 95 has been dubbed the "mystic chord" by Scriabine's pupils.

Ex. 97    CHOPIN, Op. 11

C        V Harmony

# Chapter VIII

## MODERN NINTHS, ELEVENTHS AND THIRTEENTHS
### (Secondary)

The question is frequently asked, "Why all the dissonance in our modern music?" Doubtless one important reason for this is the constant desire for new and untried harmony.* Perhaps the most beautiful chord of all time is the ordinary dominant ninth, major and minor, which Wagner exploited in such splendor in his music dramas. The supertonic ninth unless altered is more dissonant, as are also any of these other ninths: I, III, VI, and IV. Nevertheless they are some of the chords on the list that remain for the coming generations to use.

Naturally it is much more difficult for the musician to become a composer at the present time than it has been in the past. For illustration: a composer of twenty-five years ago would have harmonized the passage below in the following way:

*Leo Ornstein says, "No generation can fully express itself through the conventions of an earlier period."

But now it would seem less trite to write in the following way: Ex 99

Here we are using first (a) a major triad, major seventh, and major ninth; and second (b) a minor triad, minor seventh, and major ninth; two entirely different ninth chords, both equally good.

It is the duty, perhaps, of the modern composer to use chords the interest in which is contemporaneous with him in the course of historical sequence. The dominant ninth contributions have had their day and should be tabooed more or less. The auditor who is not up-to-date in his listening might still prefer the first way, but the latter method is the fresher and newer.

So in the following, the usage of the past is shown:

Ex 100

while the future might bring this:

Ex 101
*Allegro giocoso*

especially if the program calls for playful, reckless abandon; the biting dissonance adds zest and one revels in its exotic tang.

With all these new dissonances to reckon with, it is not strange that present-day compositions should be grotesque, demoniacal, and even pandemoniacal in character.* The very materials that are left the composer suggest such treatment.†

It was rare indeed to find a secondary ninth until recent years. Of the following list of chords a number are becoming quite familiar.

Ex. 102

II₉    VI₉    IV₉    III₉    I₉

‡ Ex. 103  Pelléas and Mélisande                    DEBUSSY

---

*Familiar examples in which cacophonous methods are found are *Pacific 231*, by Honegger, and *Flivver 10,000,000*, by F. S. Converse.

†Is not the bitter tang, the rudeness, the noisy audacity and even barbarism characteristic, not merely of jazz, but of modern music, a revolt against the cloying sweetness, balanced symmetry, overrefinement, and thin politeness of yesterday's music?"—William Arms Fisher. Address before the M. T. N. A. 1923.

‡A. Durand & Fils.

In the following example it will be evident that all members are essential:

**Ex. 104**

(a)

Fourth chord

Whole tone

II₁₁  IV₉  VI₁₁  II₉  V

(b)

Whole tone chords

VI₁₁  IV₉  II₇  IV₇  I₇

(c)

IV₁₁  VI₇  V₁₃  I₇  II₉  VI₉  II₁₁  IV₉

(d)

Aug.

7♭
6
5

3♯
2♯

I₁₃  VII₁₃  IV♯  VII₇

Some of the most fascinating harmony is being neglected because of the failure to include these dissonances. Naturally these chords are of little value in harmony in four-parts or even more, if employed for voices only, as it is necessary that they be placed higher than the compass of the voice; so we are now discussing instrumental harmony. In these higher discords it is necessary that some portion of the chord should be omitted, sometimes the ninth or seventh if it is major. This depends on the placement. It is not so necessary to omit the third as in the dominant formations because that member does not conflict so much with the eleventh.

Some of these secondary discords have possibilities of finer expression than the old dominant discords (the seventh and ninth) whose charm has been almost exhausted.

Again, if we are writing for instruments, the demand or desire for resolution is not so imperative. Major sevenths may frequently resolve upward, and resolution by substitution (of one voice for another, as the bearer of the resolution) should be used freely.

In some ways the seventh has required the downward resolution where the higher dissonances have not; for instance, the ninth frequently resolves up to the third, if the resolution is on the same root.

Ex. 105

When one is employing many parts in the chord, almost any diatonic leading will bring about a resolution by substitution or else by applying some one of the already-accepted theories of resolution. After a context full of secondary discords, the plain dominant seventh sounds very much out of place, and in such a situation a part of the whole-tone dominant discussed in Chapter XIV seems appropriate.

Other dominant substitutes are possible; one of these is founded on the whole-tone subtonic. Cyril Scott uses this cadence in one of his *Technical Studies*. Note the progression in the bass.

\* Ex. 106   Technical Studies

CYRIL SCOTT

*Elkins & Co., Ltd.*

Cértain consecutive fifths of an agreeable type, and consecutive seconds and sevenths sometimes appear when many parts are brought together. This inevitable result may be an aid to the better understanding of the reason for the inclusion of such progressions in modern music. Consecutive seconds have been used between different positions of the same fundamental harmony Ex. 107 (b).

Ex 107

Percy Grainger, in his *Mock Morris,* makes use of this interesting supertonic eleventh chord which we usually consider an impossibility.

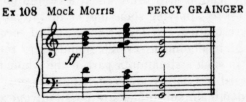

Ex 108 Mock Morris    PERCY GRAINGER

Perhaps another writer will later use the chord as in Ex. 109. The theory student of the future will have many more highly developed formations to master.

Ex.109

## CHAPTER IX

## THE DECEPTIVE RESOLUTION OF CHORDS

Perhaps the most effective means of acquiring new and interesting harmonic progressions would be to resolve chords, not in the accustomed ways, but by leading them into new and untried fields, for them—a realm hitherto unexplored. The *deceptive resolution* has been applied to the dominant in the familiar progression, dominant to submediant; but this general process may be applied to any dissonant chord and with stimulating results. In Ex. 110 we see a few of the methods of resolving the secondary seventh chord *d-f-a-c*, not to the dominant of *C major* or *C minor*, but to some chord more distant.

Ex. 110

This process can be applied to the Neapolitan resolution or augmented chords in the following ways, among others:

Ex. 111

73

**Ex. 112**

The deceptive progression from dominant harmony possesses unlimited possibilities. Several varieties are suggested here, even to the employment of the dominant thirteenth in attractive leadings.

**Ex. 113**

From Dominant thirteenth to other unrelated chords.

## The Augmented Fourth Relationship
### to the Dominant

The relationship of the regular dominant and of other dominant chords built on the augmented fourth or diminished fifth below is employed so frequently that an explanation of this method seems necessary.

The two chords have two notes in common, and with the two binding tones it is a simple matter to move the parts so as to include the full chord. Notice in Ex. 115 (a) the connection of the two dominants, also Ex. 115 (b) where the second one is a dominant ninth.

This is one of Scriabine's overworked devices,—potentially a most glorious means of expression, but one which soon "accumulates" a monotony. He used the relationship as an exclusive method throughout some of his compositions.

**Ex. 114**  Etude, Op. 56, № 4

A. SCRIABINE

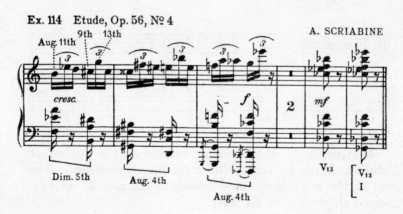

Here he makes use of the eleventh and thirteenth until one scarcely knows whether they are real chord members or appoggiaturas.

A few of the variations of such methods are shown in Ex. 115 (c), (d), (e), and (f).

A more fascinating study than that of progressions of this

class cannot be conceived; the imagination can easily move on to other and varied solutions.

While the chord on $d^b$ may be the dominant of the Neapolitan of IV ($g^b$, $b^b$, $d^b$, in the key of $C$), yet it illustrates a special device that is so intimately connected with the keynote, both through the Neapolitan of the tonic and its use (by Scriabine and others) in the relationship of the augmented fourth from the dominant, that it might have a special analysis.

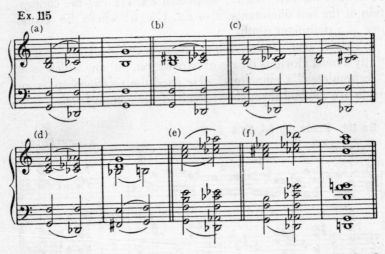

Ex. 115

It is probable that Scriabine arrived at his method of building chords by fourths through this relationship. The root of the new chord could belong to the first as an augmented eleventh (See Ex. 114).

## CHAPTER X

# THE SEMITONAL SCALE AND CHORDS
## (TWELVE NOTES)

### RECENT METHODS IN SECURING A MORE HOMOGENEOUS CONCORD BETWEEN DIATONIC AND CHROMATIC ELEMENTS

A fairly well established idea that meets with approval is the contention that all triads, seventh chords, ninth chords, etc., founded on all chromatic steps of the scale may be brought within the range of one central tonic. This is by far the most valuable idea for the future theorist and composer to develop that has been put forward in recent years.

### IN MAJOR KEYS

Take, for example, the following major triads as usable in the key of *C major*:

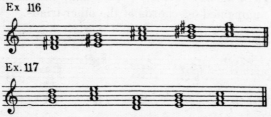

We have taken all the minor triads and the diminished chord and converted them into major chords. Any chord may be used in the manner of a dominant; so that if we apply the test here, we shall find it may resolve to the triad a fifth below, thereby bringing in as the temporary tonics: V, VI, II, III and IV, shown in Ex. 117.

By this process we secure apparent modulations to the keys next related to *C*, but the mere appearance of two chords of a relative key does not usually imply a modulation, unless one follows the series with a final complete cadence in that key. So we assume that each major or minor triad in each key can have its own dominant, a generally accepted theory at the present time.

If all triads (major or minor) are apparently usable as though *temporary* tonics, then a theory of this kind might be evolved about the triads on the flat side. Take for example the Neapolitan triad, $d^b$, $f$, $a^b$, in Ex. 118.

Ex 118

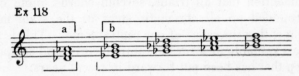

If this is the Neapolitan of *C Major*, then the other triads shown in Ex. 118 may also be Neapolitans of the triads of ii, iv, v, vi respectively. The same argument holds with regard to the augmented chords of these various triads. The augmented 6-5 of the key of *C* is $a^b$, $c$, $e^b$, and $f^\sharp$, shown in Ex. 119 with the augmented 6-5 chords of the other triads.

Ex. 119

Aug. $_5^6$ of  I          V          VI          II          III          IV

Naturally all other augmented chords can be included: i.e., augmented 6, augmented 6-4-3, and augmented 6-4-3 with doubly augmented octave.

## Dominant Formations

So far only the dominant triads have been used as the basis of the present process; naturally the sevenths and ninths may be added to these dominant triads. To the dominants shown in Ex. 116 we may add, then, the following ones:

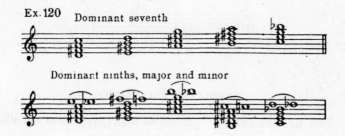

## DOMINANT FORMATIONS
### IN MINOR KEYS

### *C minor*

In the minor keys we find different dominants available. With the III chord this $v^9$ may be used:

With the VI, the following dominant:

and with the VII with lowered root, the following one:

The dominant of the Neapolitan may likewise be used:*

Ex. 124

N.

### Neapolitan Dominants

This process can be applied to all Neapolitans of other triads, the former acting as temporary tonics.

Ex. 125　C minor

Neapolitan of III　and　V₉　　Neapolitan of IV　and　V₉

Some of these appear out of place in major keys, but there is an increasing tendency to mix major and minor, so this possibility virtually resolves itself to the fact that chords may be used, interchangeably, in major or minor. Naturally this would be one of the last processes before moving on to atonality. So we find that all chords can be brought under the influence of one tonic if so desired.

The resolving of each dominant to its secondary tonic is not obligatory. It may move from one ninth to another, or directly to the home tonic, or to the home dominant before the tonic (some of the varieties are shown in Ex. 126). This method raises the other half-steps to a position commensurate with the diatonic ones and the scale is no longer chromatic, but semitonal (Ex. 53).

*See Chopin, Prelude, op. 28, No. 20, near the end.

Ex. 126

Here we are using seven dominant major ninths,* showing preparation and resolution. These are all possible in the one key of *C major* without any implication of a modulation. Naturally there are other methods introducing and resolving these, but this example will show a few of the ways and means of employing chords that are not in common use in the connections shown, suggestions of which possibilities, however, one finds in some compositions of recent years.

The consecutive perfect fifths in the two lowest voices are of an agreeable sort; in fact any fifths caused by movements of consecutive ninths are admissible.† In Ex. 126, (h) and (i), the use of minor ninths is shown.

We must remember that artificially-made diminished seventh chords (the four upper notes of the dominant minor ninth chord) for each triad have been in use by classic composers since the time of Mozart. It is then only one step further to add a major third under each, and secure the coveted ninth.

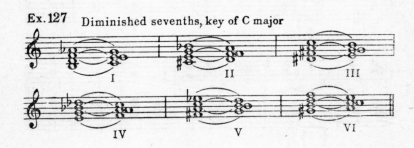

Ex. 127   Diminished sevenths, key of C major

To these diminished sevenths we will add the major thirds below to complete the ninths:

*Edward J. Dent points out that "Dissonances are built upon every degree of the chromatic scale (each degree acquiring the function of a dominant); the predominance of the dominant and tonic of the old system is extinguished and new laws have to be discovered empirically to cope with the situation."

†These bassoon or 'cello fifths are particularly effective.

Ex 128

## LATER METHODS IN SECURING SEMITONAL FEELING
## WITHOUT DIATONIC IMPLICATIONS

The preceding chromatic notes are largely diatonic in their origin. If one wished it to appear as though the twelve notes* making up a chromatic scale were *bona fide* scale members, he must not use them as passing-notes between diatonic ones, but as real chord members.

Ex. 129   Pièce heroïque                                CESAR FRANCK

The excerpt from Cesar Franck's *Pièce Héroïque* affords one of the best examples of the semitonal writing that we have. The piece is in *B minor,* but the third chord is a *B major* chord, and the fourth chord an augmented triad on *b♭*. In the second measure we have the dominant of *B minor* restored, but with a minor third; the *B minor* key feeling is recovered, but in a modal way. The major thirds at the top assist in securing this semitonal feeling without in this case

*"The whole twelve notes are demanded, not in any order of precedence, not with any real or imagined grades of dissonance, but as a homogeneous medium in which all intervals, all scales, and all chords have equal prescriptive validity."
—*The New Music,* by George Dyson.

making it appear as though it were connected with the whole-tone scale, as major thirds frequently do. In this passage we have no feeling that the *B major* chord has anything to do with *E minor*, subdominant minor to *B minor*. If the octave is divided into twelve equal parts it admits of successions of intervals and chords equal in quality. New harmonic connections of a most striking nature may be secured in this way, such as those in Ex. 129. This may be effectuated by employing some line of progression, usually in the bass, of exactly equal steps. So we can see how the parallel movement of chords as shown in Ex. 51 and 53 may be a part of this system, and how in the excerpt from Ravel's *Valses Nobles* the bass progressing by fourths helps to secure this desired unity.

Ex. 130 Valses nobles                                    RAVEL

If we include the whole set of half-steps in one scale, the task of uniting them is a difficult one. We are so accustomed to regarding the chromatic intervals in such a series as leading-tones of new keys on the dominant side or minor sevenths of dominant chords on the subdominant side, that any other leading seems paradoxical. There should be a constant impression of what the tonic keynote would be (the gift of "absolute" pitch would be an advantage here). We are now assuming that we are not working in the atonal or polytonal way. The key feeling may be retained by employing certain scale lines in the melody or by using a sequence of chords whose possible ultimate leading to a tonic is at once evident.

On the other hand, definite key feeling may be nullified by the use in the main of major triads, the bass progressing in major thirds downward, a means by which one has numerous altered chords without an implied modulation. The composer should then usually avoid dominant sevenths, for they suggest a definite key, and therefore might imply a modulation. An occasional augmented chord, which is always ambiguous, might be used.

There is a certain affinity between the whole-tone scale and the duodecuple because the former one has six notes and the latter twelve. The whole-tone scale might be regarded as the arpeggio of the duodecuple scale and the intervening degrees the passing-notes. (See Glossary.)

In the duodecuple system we find a new tonal center, the diminished fifth or augmented fourth from the tonic (it may be used as such, but is not obligatory). Scriabine adopts at times but two bass tones, an augmented or diminished fifth apart. If we count the half-steps, we find the tonal center in the key of $C$ to be on $f^\sharp$ or $g^\flat$, so a new dominant may be founded on this step. See Ex. 131 for an instance of the use of this "new dominant" center.

One finds occasionally passages of equal intervals in the older composers' works; their use, however, was mostly confined to certain cadenzas or transitional passages. See Chopin Op. 9, No. 3, near the end.

Ex. 131   Organ Piece                                    H. A. M.

*cresc.*

### SEMITONAL CHORDS APPLIED TO EXOTIC SCALES

A method slightly different from the preceding and yet somewhat in keeping may be worked out by harmonizing exotic scales, as shown in Ex. 132. This yields interesting harmonic material borrowed from the semitonal scale. The harmony is not necessarily new, but it is combined in new and refreshing ways because of the scale line above it.

If we take the modal scales, or any artificial, Oriental, or whole-tone scale, and harmonize them with consecutive tonics of various keys, we secure a type of harmony that utilizes the half-steps, suggesting not the chromatic scale but a scale of twelve notes. In this, the flats and sharps are raised to a position of equality with the diatonic notes. When we speak of consecutive tonics here, we refer to major and minor triads artificially produced from other triads, not in a modulatory sense.

The scale line in the soprano points to a definite keynote, so the ultimate leading is felt to be undisturbed. Major triads are introduced in the most unexpected ways by this process, with an effect which is very similar to that of modal harmony. All musicians, and students as well, should be able to write as striking harmony as Dvořák uses in the introduction of the slow movement in the "New World" symphony. Some such method as shown above will assist.

We have undoubtedly been tied to one or two scales until we are no longer aware that there are richer harmonic resources to be employed outside. Even harmonization of the much abused whole-tone scale, not with whole-tone chords, but with whatever triads are appropriate, is beneficial. Ex. 132 (j).

Busoni has brought together, new and old, one hundred and thirteen scales.

Ex. 132

Busoni Scale

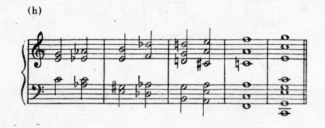

(J) Whole tone scale

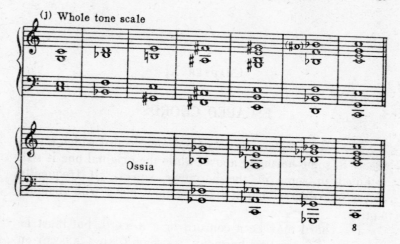

Ossia

8

## Chapter XI

## ESCAPED CHORDS*

The escaped chord is an independent chord which moves freely to some harmony above, while the original one is still retained in some of the harmonic voices. It frequently moves one degree, but it likewise may move with disjunct motion.

The chord may be a concord or a discord, but must be dissonant with the true harmony. It should always occur on the weak beat and should never be resolved; hence the name, "escaped." It may be prepared, or introduced freely. There should be a relationship somewhere, even though quite distant.

If the chord moves to a chord within the diatonic range, it is called unitonic, and outside (chromatic) it is called polytonic.

In Ravel's piano piece *Les Grande vents venus d'outremer* we find an illustration of this method; also in Strauss' *Elektra* some of these chords may probably be accounted for along the lines of polytonality. Much depends on the spacing and tone colour.

## Pedal Chords

Instead of the single "pedal" we now meet with pedal chords which are sustained against chords much as in Ex. 133.

*See *Traite d'Harmonie ultramoderne*, by Louis Villermin, for a more exhaustive study of this method.

Perhaps the best illustration of this can be found in Strauss'
*Rosenkavalier.* The following table is self-explanatory:

## CHAPTER XII

# THE SUPERDOMINANT

A rather remarkable experiment with the dominant might be carried out in the following way, as shown in Ex. 135, a process which may help to systematize a harmonic chimera that doubtless numerous musicians are trying to allocate: First, from the bass upward include the following in the order given: root, minor seventh, major third, minor ninth, augmented fifth, and augmented ninth. Resolve this chord to the tonic with a major seventh added in the soprano. Notice that all voices except the bass move by half-steps (Ex. 135, 1). Second, use the same dominant chord as above, but with a diminished fifth added (Ex. 135, 2). Third, a chord of the root, minor seventh, major third, augmented fifth, minor ninth, diminished fifth, and augmented ninth, resolving to the tonic with a seventh in the soprano (Ex. 135, 3). Fourth, a chord of the root, minor seventh, major third, diminished fifth, augmented fifth, and minor third, resolving to the tonic with a major sixth added in the soprano (Ex. 135, 4). Fifth, the same dominant chord as the preceding one, with a minor ninth added (Ex. 135, 5). Sixth, a chord of the root, minor seventh, major third, augmented fifth, augmented ninth, augmented eleventh, and major seventh, resolving to the tonic with a major seventh and major ninth added in middle voice (Ex. 135, 6). Seventh, a chord of the root, minor seventh, major seventh, major third, augmented fifth, augmented eleventh (doubled), major seventh (fifteenth partial), and augmented ninth, resolving to the tonic with major seventh and major ninth added (Ex. 135, 7). Eighth, a chord of the root, minor seventh, major ninth, major third, aug-

mented fifth, major seventh, augmented ninth, and augmented
eleventh, resolving to the tonic with the major seventh and
major ninth added (Ex. 135, 8 ).   Ninth, a chord of the major
third (in the bass), root, minor seventh, major ninth, augmented fifth, root, major eleventh, perfect fifth, major
seventh, augmented ninth and augmented eleventh, resolving
to the tonic with major sixth, major ninth and major seventh
added (Ex. 135, 9 ).   This latter one is a veritable sky-scraper,
including ten different notes in the chord, and yet not sounding disagreeable.*   The secret of this effectiveness is due to
the fact that almost all voices move to their resolutions by
half steps.†   Some of these can be inverted with the more
unusual notes in the bass.   Ex. 135, (a), (b), (c), (d), (e).

With minor and augmented fifths and ninths, and possibly minor thirds and major sevenths added to the dominants,
the future of the theorist and composer will be a busy one.
The final tonic under such conditions shimmers and glows
with an alluring charm.

Ex. 135

*Leo Ornstein goes so far as to say, "All tones, under intellectual and emotional
stress, can be incorporated with each other."

†"Any two or three chords, no matter how dissonant, which can be resolved into
the same chord, may be played together."—Observation by the well-known
musical theorist, Hugo Leichtentritt, in *Modern Music*, on "Schönberg and
Tonality."

After an analysis of conditions as shown in Ex. 135, we discover that in any ordinary major dominant ninth, if the chord is sufficiently dispersed, the following alterations of the common-chord parts may appear together with their unaltered selves, provided these altered notes are placed in the extreme upper parts: first, the minor third or its equivalent, the augmented ninth; second, the diminished fifth and augmented fifth or their equivalents, the augmented eleventh and minor thirteenth (the natural fifth usually omitted); third, the major seventh or its equivalent, the diminished octave;

and fourth, the minor and augmented ninth if separated by at least an octave (major ninth omitted).

The manner of writing these notes depends on their resolutions. In the chord shown in Ex. 135, ₉, we find all but two notes of the chromatic scale included. This chord is exceptional, but various forms may be constructed to include these unusual additions to the dominant.

Maurice Ravel is a composer who uses some of these additions, especially the minor third (see *Daphnis et Chloe*). His harmony is deeply rooted in tradition, there being no striving after atonality or even an approach to it.

If one is still disposed to build his chords in the old way, by superimposed thirds, he must, after the thirteenth is added, begin the series over again and make his alterations there, building the chords empirically as regards size of interval, for example:

**Ex. 136**

Naturally this looks absurd for memorization; but it is only necessary to remember that any part of a dominant major ninth chord may appear, in the same chord, with its lowered self (except the further lowered minor seventh) and with its raised self if a fifth, seventh (now raised to major) or ninth, provided the spacing is separative enough to neutralize the harshness of the dissonance.

Chords as shown in Ex. 135 are appoggiatura-like in effect. A harmonic artifice of this type should be used only by those who are able to write in different simultaneous harmonic planes; therefore a well contrived form of orchestration is of paramount importance. The harshness of these dissonances is neutralized in this way. "The significance of a chord in a musical scheme resides not in the notes it consists of but in its functions, in the part it plays within the scheme."—CALVOCORESSI, in *Musical Criticism*. The degree of dissonance depends on the context. To satisfy this desire for dissonance, we find in use final harmony containing complete tonic and dominant in one chord (see Ex. 137). It would be absurd to ignore all previous implications of a composition by ending with a simple complacent triad, as if to say, "I herewith repudiate all previous assertions."

In the chords given in Ex. 136 we find that the dissonances are suggested by the harmonic series.* The $c^{\#}$ represents the eleventh harmonic; the $f^{\#}$, the fifteenth harmonic; the $d^{\#}$ can represent the thirteenth harmonic; and the $a^{\#}$ a harmonic, number nineteen, that is beyond the series shown in Ex. 9.

In the final tonics of some of the dominants in Ex. 135 we find the tonic and dominant together representing the tonic (See also Ex. 114).

Ex. 137   Etude, Op. 56, № 4                    SCRIABINE

*"Our music has sprung from the patient, incessant, and progressive penetration into the law of resonance, that is to say, from the successive exploitation of the *octave*, the *fifth* and the *fourth* (ninth to twelfth century), the *third* (thirteenth to sixteenth century), the *seventh* (seventeenth and eighteenth century), the *major ninth*, the *augmented fifth,* and the *perfect eleventh* (nineteenth and twentieth centuries) . . . . this evolution . . . . constitutes, at the same time, the only true justification of musical art."—*The Evolution of Music*, Alfredo Casella.

## CHAPTER XIII

# PASSING CHORDS AND POLYTONALITY
## (POLYHARMONIC)

Another modern device is the passing chord. George Dyson says, in his book, *The New Music*, "The melodic threads of the contrapuntist have become composite streams of harmony, and these streams may approach and recede, coalesce or clash, just as did the individual parts of polyphony." This process had its early prototype in the organum of the early writers (Ex. 138).

Ex.138    Tonus Protus

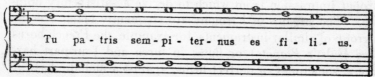

These same diaphonic methods can be traced into modern music, e.g., Debussy's *la Cathédrale engloutie*, and Holst's *Planets: Mars*. Probably the best modern example of such a method, which might better be called polyharmonic than polytonal, is shown in Stravinsky's *Pétrouchka* (Ex. 140). But compositions have become much more complex, even to the combining of two or more keys at the same time (See Goossens' *Gorgoyles*, where he uses different key signatures for right and left hands).

Sir Henry Wood says, in his article on "Orchestral Color and Values" in *A Dictionary of Modern Music and Musicians*, "The fact is that the color obtained from the orchestra, but not from the piano, can entirely change harmonic ideas.

Thus in the modern orchestra the most violent harmonic clashes, the juxtaposition of several keys at once, can give perfect aesthetic pleasure."

The final chord in one of our modern compositions is something like this:

Ex. 139

The critical student should realize the medium, then, before he condemns the harmony.    The piano score will not give the proper impression from which to derive a satisfactory opinion.    The streams of harmony are frequently taken over by a group of similar instruments, for example, the French horns (see Holst's *Planets*) or flutes in three and four-part harmony, sometimes in perfect fifths, against a melodic bass or other sustained parts; and sometimes with this is included the harp, which casts a magic glow over the whole picture.

\* Ex. 140  Petrouchka                                   STRAVINSKY

Edward Burlingame Hill, in his book, *Modern French Music*, applies the word polyharmony in place of polytonal-

*It has been said of Stravinsky, "His different harmonies occurring simultaneously are made clear by an element of contact which is endowed by all the virtues of a tonic, fulfilling the function of a pole from which the harmonies themselves radiate."—ERNEST ANSERMET.

ity. It is probable that each of these terms has its own place. Ex. 140 is a clear illustration of polyharmony not polytonality.

## INTERPLAY OF THE SONORITIES

We have here reached a stage of musical development where the ear can no longer function on a single aural line. It is necessary to fix our attention upon two or three of these lines of progression at the same time.

The illustration from Bantock's song, *The Guardian Angel*, is a fine example of this double listening.

Ex. 141  The Guardian Angel

BANTOCK

Two independent harmonic movements are here contrasted, regardless of the dissonances resulting.

If this were written for orchestra, the clashing effect of the dissonances could be entirely eliminated; in fact they would be agreeable by reason of the contrasting colors. One authority describes such methods as the "interplay of the sonorities."

## POLYTONALITY

To those who are diametrically opposed to polytonality this suggestion from Alfredo Casella will elucidate the harmonic problem somewhat: "There are still many who

*Boosey & Co.

wrongly consider polytonality* to be something purely arbitrary . . . . They ought, on the contrary, to consider that the introduction in simultaneity of diatonic fragments was a natural result of the employment in succession of continuous modulating passages, and polytonality was to come sooner or later as a result of this abuse of modulation."

Polytonality subdivides into two species: harmonic and melodic. The harmonic species is that which superimposes and interweaves chords belonging to different tonalities. In this process, chords belonging to different keys are sounded together, but always with the idea of the natural and indispensable basis of the diatonic scale. Melodic polytonality superimposes two or more melodies of diverse tonalities. This is a much more difficult process and has been successfully accomplished by Alfredo Casella in his *Pagine di Guerra.*

Polytonal music is the antithesis of atonal. A fixed tonality somewhere is essential. This process is usually connected with different quintal planes:

Ex. 142

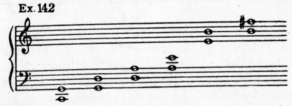

The first, or home tonic is definitely established, and to this in an adjoining quintal plane the second part is added. One's attention being called to the new part or parts, the original one retreats into the background, and yet one is still

---

*"If eventually the physical displeasure caused by the clash of polytonal combinations proves such that only an effort of mind and will-power enables a listener to endure it, for that listener, be he a critic or not, the problem is solved. The fact that combinations which were intolerable are nowadays pleasurable does not imply that there is no limit to the ear's tolerance. And if it turns out that polytonal music is not meant for the ear, and does not stimulate the imagination, polytonal music will have to go."—CALVOCORESSI in *Musical Criticism.*

conscious of its primordial importance. Each new addition
may be considered in the same way until the five different
planes are joined. Indeed, at one place in Gustav Holst's
*Ode on a Grecian Urn,* this actually occurs, making the complete chord build by perfect fifths.

This is by far the most daring innovation that modern
composers have attempted, and it is likewise the movement
that musicians are most averse to accepting. Some of the
most extraordinary situations and moods may be depicted by
such methods, leading one to the point of being terrified,
causing one at times to shudder at its catastrophic power.
However, musicians will be more favorable to this phase of
modernism as they become more cognizant of its value.

The quintal planes alluded to are also utilized from a
central point outward in both directions, so that we secure
what is called a mirroring, the upper major chords reflecting
the minor below.

Ex. 143

Numerous triads may be constructed from these chords.
Parts may be selected from these separate planes and com-
bined. The connection is remote. (See Louis Villermin's
*Traité d' Harmonie.*)

Ex. 144

Louis Villermin, in his *Traite d'Harmonie ultramoderne*, gives an extended list of a mixture of these combinations until it would appear that every chord would be included. From the chords in Ex. 143 we may assemble the following scales:

**Ex. 145**

This accounts for the appearance of major and minor chords together. In Ex. 146 and 147, we find two simple experiments in this line.

## HORIZONTAL LISTENING
### COMPOSITE STREAMS OF HARMONY

During the past fifty years our listening has been mainly perpendicular.  With the discovery of the vast harmonic resources, our attention has been largely concentrated on the chord, but now composers are making use of what might be called harmonic counterpoint.  They develop contrasting groups of harmony in different planes, sometimes in two, more frequently in three or four.  For a simple piano illustration of this in two composite parts and pedal, see Eugène Goossens' *Promenade,* from his collection for piano, *Kaleidoscope,* Op. 18.

Ex. 148   Promenade from"Kaleidoscope", Op. 18

GOOSSENS

Above the pedal are two streams of harmony which occasionally harmonize and at other times disagree.  The lower part pursues a definitely established course, the dissonances always being the same, i.e., major sevenths and augmented fourths (one diminished fifth), the upper part having a melody previously stated, but here independently harmonized, mainly with perfect fourths and major sixths. In writing in this way, the harmony can be of almost any description so long as there is a binding element somewhere. One should listen horizontally, and incidental clashes should be ignored (See also Ex. 38).

Another fine illustration of this method is pictured in the following excerpt from a compressed score of the last movement of Percy Grainger's Suite, *In a Nutshell.*

**\* Ex. 149** Suite, "In a Nutshell"

GRAINGER

This fragment prepared by the composer himself combines five separate streams. The piano part descends in chromatic progression of dominant sevenths while the woodwind parts include the ninth and eleventh of this dominant in double octaves. The French horns have their own harmonic plane, as do the upper strings and lower basses. This is a

\*G. Schirmer, Inc.

fine, clear, and concise illustration of this process which so few thoroughly understand.

In his later compositions, Grainger makes use of numerous attractive percussion instruments, not of the drum type, but percussion instruments of definite pitch. These instruments, manufactured by Deagan of Chicago, carry out the xylophone, glockenspiel, and celesta idea to a most remarkable degree. Some of these new qualities are the very timbres necessary to use for softening the upper partials, and to make complex harmony more attractive.

In the following example we find a clear illustration of two well-organized harmonic streams, the movements of which are so well arranged that they can be accepted *ipso facto* by all, notwithstanding temporary clashes. Here we find not passing-notes and embellishing notes but passing chords and embellishing chords, not against a single bass note, as in the classic days (See Beethoven Sonata, Op. 2, No. 3, last movement), but against a complete chord.

This is only a natural development of past resources. To quote the *Musical Pilgrim* on Debussy and Ravel, by F. H. Shea, "However experimental or revolutionary a composer may seem at the outset, it will eventually be found that his innovations are, after all, only the logical development of resources already explored. The experiments of our age again become the normal stock in trade of the next."

Ex. 150  Nature Poem, Op. 25, No. 3        EUGENE GOOSSENS

*J. & W. Chester, Ltd.

## CHAPTER XIV

## WHOLE-TONE DOMINANT CHORDS

This seemingly mysterious subject which our harmony books systematically avoid, and yet, at the same time, pass judgment upon as being of little importance, will be first considered in a somewhat exhaustive way because of its close connection with the new harmonies discussed in later chapters. While bringing considerable complexity into both the writing and reading of compositions employing such harmony, yet, when one accustoms himself to the process, it becomes quite easy to handle and will well repay the effort involved.

The dominant seventh at cadence points has become ineffective in the most modern harmonic contexts. We must seek to give dominant harmony more life—to rescue it from limitation to the mild tensity of the Handelian cadence.

As we all know, the process of building chords, when applied to the whole-tone scale, must be entirely different from that used with the ordinary diatonic scale, for only augmented triads appear. It is necessary to construct these empirically, i.e., without regard to an apparent system. Some of the following chord combinations (Ex. 151), all the

Ex. 151

tones of each one of which are in one or the other of the two whole-tone scales, are a result of such procedure.   See Ex. 159.

When we first observe the last eight of these chords they look quite impossible of analysis, and yet they are fairly easy to understand if properly explained.   Their main characteristic is that they contain a number of augmented intervals, being made up of two augmented triads built on adjoining degrees, but naturally, for musical reasons, more widely dispersed.

A. Eaglefield Hull, in his excellent book on *Modern Harmony* suggests that whole-tone scales are in reality *arpeggios* within the duodecuple *scale*, meaning, then, that they are notes of a chord, a theory which would seem true (note in Ex. 153, where a fragment of the *Londonderry Air* is harmonized with these chords, the final one containing all the notes of the scale, with the effect of a half-cadence.

If this is the case, then we would seem to build chords by major seconds rather than by thirds, but as, in the ordinary harmony, chords sound better spread over a wider range, so with these; therefore, they are constructed on the hit-or-miss plan, governed only by good sonority.

These chords are more nearly related to the dominant than to any other chord, or perhaps to the augmented six-four-three; but they may be tonic or dominant or belong to any key, or they may be ambiguous.    Béla Bartók, in one of his *Deux Images* for orchestra, uses one of these six-tone chords as a final tonic, — naturally not the most restful final chord, but appropriate in a special style of composition.

This last is, after all, a very logical combination if you will observe the harmonic series shown in Ex. 9.   It will be seen that the notes of the whole-tone chord are all contained therein, except that the thirteenth is less nearly approximated by tempered pitch than are the other partials concerned.

The whole-tone dominant ninth can easily be brought within the dominant range and used accordingly.   If we lower and raise the fifth of the dominant major ninth at the same time, we secure the whole-tone six-voiced dominant (if one so desires, these altered notes may be spelled, and used, as augmented eleventh and minor thirteenth).   While the term "whole-tone dominant" has never been so applied by theorists in general, it would seem well to do so because of the growing frequency of the use of this chord at cadence points.

If we take the whole-tone scale, in this case the one which makes up the dominant chord, Ex. 154, and adjust the voices, giving them the required nomenclature, we secure the whole-tone dominant ninth.

Ex. 154

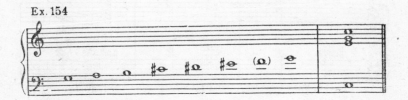

Ex. 155

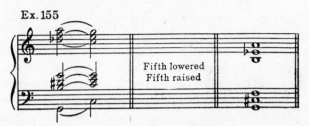

Fifth lowered
Fifth raised

For analytical purposes it might be better to write this chord with raised and lowered fifth, but it has been and will be written in various ways (here $c^{\#}$ and $e^{b}$—augmented eleventh and minor thirteenth); or the chord may be constructed by superimposed fourths; Ex. 152 or 155.

The prevailing impression seems to be that because whole-tone melody has become more or less taboo, owing to monotony, whole-tone harmony should likewise be condemned. This, however, should not be the case. Whole-tone chords can be used very effectively with chromatic melody. It is doubtless true that this harmony will be an important part of our future technic, as soon as all are aware of its value and have a working knowledge of its usefulness and an appreciation of its beauty.

This harmony was a most natural result in the development of music. Chords already contained augmented fourths and sixths; with the advent of chords with augmented fifth, the whole-tone chords naturally were evolved.

Not only can all five inversions be freely used (Ex. 156) and resolved in their different ways to the tonic of the key,

Ex. 156

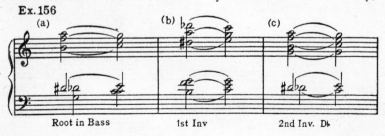

(a)        (b)        (c)

Root in Bass        1st Inv        2nd Inv. D♭

|          |          |          |
|----------|----------|----------|
| 2nd Inv. D♯ | 3rd Inv. | 4th Inv. |

but also the bass-note of each inversion may be the root of a chord representing a dominant of a different key and resolved accordingly, as shown in Ex. 157.   The chords shown at (b), (c), (d), (e), and (f) in Ex. 156 are the enharmonic equivalents of, and therefore sound the same as the dominants of *E*, *G♭*, *A♭*, *B♭*, and *D major*, respectively, as shown in Ex. 157. Therefore, these chords are extremely useful for modulatory purposes.

**Ex.157**

In them we find augmented intervals (the whole-tone scale is largely productive of such), the augmented fourth and sixth* in the augmented six-four-three chord being important parts of the whole-tone scale.   All that is lacking in this original chord to complete the scale is a major second (major ninth)

*Augmented sixth as enharmonic equivalent of the minor seventh.

and an augmented fifth, both counted from the keynote (Ex. 158). The next evolutionary process has been the addition of these two intervals.

**Ex.158**

Aug. $\frac{6}{4}$

As one may observe from the following example, there are only two different whole-tone scales. Consequently, there are only two different whole-tone chords of six notes, (a) and (b); but, of course, they may be written in numerous ways.

**Ex.159**

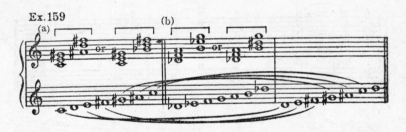

The third scale in Ex. 159 is the same as the first; in a whole-tone scale any one of the notes may be the keynote, or there may be no keynote at all.

A clever way to acquire proficiency in the use of these chords is to begin with an augmented triad in each hand, then move by contrary motion, chromatically. Every alternate chord will be the whole-tone dominant, and the intermediate chord simply an augmented triad. By playing these in the upper octaves with various degrees of touch and volume, their striking beauty will be discovered.

Ex.160

In Chapter XVIII it will be shown how these chords **may** act as resolutions for the new chords built by fourths.

In the use of whole-tone harmony, some very peculiar effects in the movement of voices are possible in consecutive seconds (Ex. 162). In Ex. 161 the five voices move in **paral**-lel motion where three sets of major thirds appear.

Ex.161

The variety of ways in which these chords may be combined is almost beyond computation, and yet there are only two six-note whole-tone chords. In the next four examples one will observe the apparent simultaneous progression of dominant 4-2 chords; that is, dominants with seventh in the bass and fifth omitted. These are used in canonical form. In Ex. 162 the three move in similar motion and finally resolve on a whole-tone chord (this can always be determined by the presence of all members of one scale in the chord). In this case, however, it has not the dominant feeling, but probably a tonic one because of its location in the passage.

Ex. 162

In Ex. 163 we have a canon in four composite streams in contrary motion, that is, one moves in a general downward direction, the other three upward, all chromatically, again ending in a whole-tone chord. When all voice groups have once started, we have, on the accents, whole-tone chords, and on the other beats simply augmented triads.

Ex. 163

Ex. 164 consists entirely of whole-tone chords, but they lack one note, and hence are five-voice harmony, except the chord at the end of the second measure, where the two voice groups double each other. At the end there is a plain minor triad.

Ex. 164

Ex. 165 (a) is a five voice-group canon in parallel motion. All the chords in the second, third and fourth measures are six-note whole-tone chords. Because of the dominant 4-2 position, the first chord of each pair might be classed as a dominant and the other as a tonic. In measure three, Ex. 165 (a), we have simultaneously five dominant sevenths, each represented by three notes.

Ex. 165 (a)

It is undoubtedly true that polytonal music has for one of its generators the whole-tone scale. In the harmonization, in Ex. 166 and 167, of the familiar folk-song *Yankee Doodle*, one will observe that it is written in six different keys which may be played together with no ill effect.

Not only this melody, but any good diatonic one may be so treated. It seems almost paradoxical that such a thing is possible, and yet one does not have to be a radical modernist to accept it. A serious study of these chords on the part of theorists and musicians will yield valuable results. When we add the varied colors of the orchestra to these harmonies, the effect is convincing. Many criticisms are brought to bear

Ex. 166    Folk-song (Yankee Doodle)
In Six Keys

Ex 167

The same together for Piano

on the whole-tone scale theory because of its artificiality.   It is probable that the whole-tone scale came not directly through melody but through harmony; therefore it was inevitable that such a series should develop.   The author does not believe that Debussy, Moussorgsky, or others contrived to construct an artificial scale, even though they might have been entirely justified in so doing if they had had sufficient melodic or harmonic reasons.*   A most striking illustration of these dominants in parallel motion is shown at Ex. 165 (b) and (c).   Can one find a more agreeable allocation of chord members?

Whole-tone harmonies, however, are apt to produce atonal relations because of their undiatonic connections, and then, thus freed, the product acquires a "Puck-like" buffoonery that no humorous music outside of such relations can approach.   At other times, its implications are of the most remote sort, not at all associated with previous experiences. These extraneous types can be expressed in no other way than to call them exotic.

The whole-tone chords and scales have done more to break the fetters of diatonicism, thus creating a new impulse for further constructive composition, than any other element since Wagner's virile modulations.   We must not assume that Debussy exhausted their possibilities, even though some have claimed so.   As a continuous idiom, whole-tone writing is monotonous, but as a constructive element in atonal writing it is a new source of material.

---

*"  . . . . the right to adopt or to create scales is now claimed by many composers, of whom some, mayhap, exercise this right by dint of sheer mechanical ingenuity."—*Musical Criticism*, Calvocoressi.

## CHAPTER XV

PROCESSES THAT VITIATE DIATONIC KEY FEELING

Whole-tone chords, as we found in Chapter XIV, are not very adaptable to the diatonic keys; there is too much disparity between each chord and its tonic. We therefore find that they have been employed in music of an exotic kind such as that of Debussy and other French composers.

These chords and parts of them were used in parallel motion, possibly because it was so difficult to find appropriate resolution chords; this was known as the impressionistic method. This type of harmony has lost its interest, or at least the tang is not strong enough for present-day taste. More piquancy is desired. The whole-tone dominant alone is not enough.

As this chord represents half the notes of the duodecuple scale, the next step is to combine notes from both of the whole-tone scales in part as one desires, if more "klang" is wanted.

Though one of these whole-tone chords, individually, is suggestive, in part, of a diatonic principle, the alternate chord or a part of it, of the opposite semitonally associated whole-tone scale, combined with it, will obliterate the tonal implications of the former and will not be able to establish any possible diatonic remnant of tonal atmosphere of the latter.

This is the best method imaginable for destroying the old key feeling and of placing the composer in a new environment where the freer conditions surrounding him drive him to speak a newer, more euphonious language, because of the new descriptive powers of tone-speech. The one great desire in modern composition is to secure a manner of writing, or an atmosphere, that is in direct opposition to diatonic principles. Some are acquiring it by returning to modal writing, a most commendable method; some, by the adoption of quarter-tone methods; others, by polytonal writing; and still others, by the so-called atonal process, if atonalism is an analyzable process.

The manner of obtaining this non-tonal atmosphere is not always clear, but we are told to use the parts of a semitonal scale in a communistic way: every note approached in a manner to give equal validity to each. The ability to do this and still give the impression that one is writing real music and not the fortuitous result of a jumblingly contrived polychrome is the problem for the modern composer and theorist to solve.*†

An explanation of the twelve-note scale, with its new chordal and melodic associations involving a complete abandonment of its diatonic and chromatic implications is then the problem under discussion. The task of the modern composer is to assimilate, or to incorporate into one organic system, these divergent elements. This scale has been given the title of duodecuple.

## The Duodecuple Scale and Its Harmonies

Harmony, then, in its most complete and complex form, at the present time, is divisible into two resonant vibrating units or chords, Ex. 168 (a) and (b). The history of har-

---

*In an article by Hugo Leichtentritt in *Modern Music* he says, "It is my experience that in some cases polytonality gives the impression of two separate tonalities going along side by side, whereas in other cases, two different tonalities heard simultaneously, produce, as a result, a third tonality different from either."

†"The whole-tone scale, whether regarded as impurity of mode when it is used momentarily, or as a new scale when used more consistently, has the effect at any rate of vitiating the tonal elements in proportion to the extent of its use. Its influence is antitonal, not merely from the harmonic standpoint, but from the melodic as well."—*A comparison of the impressions at work in the rise and decline of tonality.* Geo. Dickinson.

mony in recent years includes the use of but one of these units at a time.

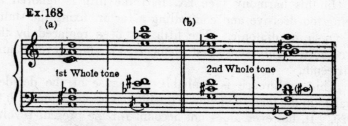

**Ex. 168**
(a)    (b)

1st Whole tone    2nd Whole tone

All possibility of evolution of either of these chords, alone, *in our present pitch system,* has practically been exhausted. The works of Debussy and Scriabine illustrate this development and exhaustion, although the latter composer has entered upon the combination of these two resonances.

The six-note whole-tone chord, arranged in fourths or otherwise is, relatively to a single whole-tone scale, a chord of rest, in the sense of complete representation of a scale of *equal* successive intervals. Scriabine used this chord in this way, and it has been accepted by others also as a means of expressing finality (Ex. 263 and 264).

In whichever whole-tone series we are writing this chord, we place the root, major third, minor seventh, major ninth, augmented eleventh (or diminished fifth), and a minor thirteenth (or augmented fifth), together as the complete harmony of one tonal medium. Ex. 168. This chord lies just outside the diatonic system but is very closely related to it because of certain characteristics similar to those of the regular dominant ninth, eleventh and thirteenth. When the perfect fifth is abandoned and an augmented fifth and diminished fifth (or augmented eleventh and minor thirteenth) are substituted for it, the new whole-tone harmony begins to assert its sovereign authority, and an entirely new music unfolds itself. It was so difficult to lead the old music into conformity or agreement with this new musical product that the entire musical idiom was almost revolutionized to make it agree with the new harmonic thought.

In this harmony (see Ex. 168) the fifth is ignored as being too decisive and controlling a factor, fixing the status of music as diatonic. The fifth has been replaced by the two more highly sensitized elements, i.e., the eleventh and thirteenth.

This preference is probably the cause of the decided change in the texture of music during the period from 1910 to 1920. It, however, does not account for the present revolution in the musical art, although it has influenced the newest development of the latter.

If the chord in Ex. 168 (a) represents the complete harmony of the more highly developed parts of one tonal system or one whole-tone scale, then we have a similar chord from the adjoining scale, a half-step higher or lower, not different from the first except in pitch. These chords may be used in fractional forms and enharmonic notations. Each one contains six different tones; the new duodecuple harmony begins, as already stated, when we start to combine the two as one complete sounding medium. This is a very satisfactory way to approach the new harmony, which employs all the way from five to twelve notes in one chord.

## Chapter XVI

## SYNTHETIC HARMONY

The combining of separate elements, sometimes radically opposed, has been carried into every line of research. The Century Dictionary and Cyclopedia says, in reference to the application of the synthetic process to acoustics, that it is the combining of two or more simple sounds of different pitch to produce or imitate a certain compound sound. This explanation applies very well to our modern harmonic methods; the difference appears in that we are now combining not simple sounds alone, but complex tonal groups, in an endeavor to produce or imitate an even more complex sound.

These intricate combinations, at times, include all the tones of a chromatic scale in one synthetic resonating structure (Ex. 169). A combination of so many tones or tonal

Ex. 169 Paeans, №3          DANE RUDHYAR

groups, together with the gorgeous color of the modern orchestra, has presented one of the marvels of the art of music.

The process of taking chords of the most diverse tonalities and synthetically metamorphosing them into one resounding body of tone is the task of the modern composer. Here we have a measure containing two chords only; the first half, a chord of nine different notes, and the second half, a chord of twelve different notes:

## RECENT DUODECUPLE RESONANCES

If the duodecuple scale is to be the basis of non-tonal music, some system of chord construction and usage should be evolved that would be reasonable and sane. As yet no system of that kind has been devised, or one might say, contrived, for one must of necessity have some hypothetical basis for such an involved structure. A scale of that type precludes the possibility of using the half-steps and whole-steps as they were used in former days; it is a scale of equal intervals like the whole-tone scale, except that the intervals are semitonal, not chromatic, because chromaticism associates each half-step with some neighboring diatonic note, and this must not be the implication in duodecuple music if the desired vagueness or the flavor of "other-worldness" is to be secured.

The best way to approach a scale of this kind is, as already stated, to divide it into two adjoining whole-tone scales, so as to give them a semitone relationship. A whole-tone scale is decidedly foreign to the old system; the harmony of the one scale will not be particularly suggestive of the diatonic principle, and naturally the harmony from the two whole-tone scales combined will obliterate the diatonic feeling entirely. Strange as this may seem at first, it gives a working basis for the newer "chordal" productions. In fact, this is the only way to approach the subject. There are evidences of such processes in much of the later music.

Ex. 170  Sketches for Piano                                    BARTOK

In Ex. 170, Bartók employs both whole-tone scales, one for each hand, in such a manner that, by the use of the pedal, the "chordal" effect is as one product.  This would be called by some a polychord.  But are we not endeavoring to combine the notes of the two adjoining whole-tone chords in our writing without being aware of it?  When these groups are separated as they are here, the feasibility of such a process is very suggestive for future investigators.

If we contend that the duodecuple scale holds all notes as having equal validity, and we attempt to divide it, we will not separate it into diatonic scales but into two *equal* divisions, the resulting scales being two whole-tone ones; so we reason that in order to gain duodecuple harmonic material, we should choose parts from each, or even all parts, if desirable, and weld them together in some effective way.  A music student with an artifice of this kind to guide him will have some control over his materials.  We then have the rule: *two interrelated whole-tone scales welded into one produce the duodecuple scale.*

The complete appearance of all members of these two

chords at one time is exceptional, but the possibility of crossing and blending parts of each into one homogeneous product is a method that is unconsciously being developed by numerous composers. This involves polytonality to some extent, but it may be pure duodecuple writing. The average polytonal writing seems to be a hodge-podge of the most improbable mixtures. The analytical method brought forward in this book, in the attempt to systematize this manner of composition, cannot, in the space here available, be set forth with the utmost fullness of detail, but it will at least give the student a foundation principle to enable him to approach modern music with some basic reason. The lure of these chords will not appear until one has studied all types of early, classical, and modern music, and comes without prejudice to the new musical shrine. There are new resonances in this harmony that will eventually appeal. See final chords in Ex. 175 (c).

## THE SYNTHETIC PROCESS

In order to release music from diatonic impressions and implications there is no better way to approach the subject than to group all tones into these two divisions.*

If we take four tones from the whole-tone scale, founded on the $c^\natural$ series, and build the chord as shown in Ex. 171 (a), and three from the second whole-tone series founded on the $d^b$ series, to produce the chord as shown in Ex. 171 (b), and then telescope the two into one chord, we have the synthetic product as shown in Ex. 171 (c).

In Ex. 171 (d), a chord of seven notes is indicated, together with its resolution, also a synthetic chord. This chord is divisible into two chords.

Some of these chords have a strong tang suggestive of percussion effects; in fact, there is a growing conviction that

*Some of Scriabine's pieces are little more than contrasting presentations of these two chords (See Ex. 114).

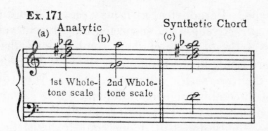

Ex. 171

(a) Analytic (b)    Synthetic Chord (c)

1st Whole- | 2nd Whole-
tone scale | tone scale

Ex. 171 (d)    Analytic

(d)

First Whole-tone | Second Whole-tone

the piano, especially, should be a dynamic instrument. It has the capacity for the display of the stinging, biting, pungent resonances so essential in modern music. Indeed the evolution of music has brought us face to face with these incisive types of harmony suggestive of the heroic.

## THE HIGHLY SENSITIZED DISSONANT HARMONY

We had supposed that the diatonic system has yielded all that was to be known of harmonic resource, but the amazingly prolific storehouse of produceable harmony inherent in the combining of the first whole-tone scale harmonies with what we shall call its semitonally co-ordinating whole-tone scale harmonies, will be serviceable for many generations of oncoming composers. This harmonic resource, to be sure, is not of the simple harmonic kind but of the alluring new dis-

sonant type.    Paradoxical as it may seem, these dissonances
have an attractiveness not suspected until recent years.    Ex.
172 gives a list of some of these combinations, the notes of
each chord being kept within one series, but the chords representing the two series alternately.    It is very difficult to
codify such combinations on a diatonic staff.    A new staff is
already a necessity.    This list of chords is not complete, as
it is exceedingly doubtful if one could exhaust the ways of
combining these notes.

### HARMONIC MATERIAL

#### EACH CHORD FROM ONE WHOLE-TONE SCALE

### (Scales Alternating)

If one can digest these chords and their successions and
find them energizing he should then try those in Ex. 173,
which are synthetic chords produced by combining the two
whole-tone series.    We thereby secure semitonal whole-tone
harmony.    We can draw a distinction between semitonal diatonic harmony and semitonal whole-tone harmony.

### HARMONY RESULTANT FROM THE COMBINATION OF BOTH WHOLE-TONE SCALES

## (Simultaneously applied)

Ex. 173.

See Ex. 84

In Ex. 173 (a), (b), (c), and (d), each has the same right-hand part; to this is added, in (a), a series of augmented fourths from the alternate whole-tone scale; in (b), a series of augmented triads; in (c) an arrangement similar to that of the right hand, in contrary motion; and in (d) a parallel progression of augmented fourths. These chords have from six to eight different tones in each chord. We can arrange for the addition of three more tones (four with the low *f*) to the eight-tone chord, to have eleven (or twelve) tones in the one chord. Ex. 173 (e). This is not at all disagreeable. Attention has already been drawn to Ex. 170 by Béla Bartók's use of ten notes which he introduces scalewise.

## Synthetic Chord Blending

We are here presenting a problem in synthetic chord blending. If we choose three chord members from one series to blend into parts from the opposite whole-tone scale, we would proceed in the following way: place the first chord in any position desirable, for instance, as in Ex. 174 (a); then write all the chord members of the alternate chord in a place where the parts may be selected from it, Ex. 174 (b); then combine in various ways to produce a highly sensitized dissonant structure, as in Ex. 174 (c).

Almost all such chords should have minor seconds together with major seconds or major sevenths and numerous augmented intervals. Sometimes after this is done one can add a bass tone or two to give it an atmosphere of mystery. These bass notes can be from either series. One should then try chords of four, five, and six notes for the starting chord and proceed to add as before. One should blend these formations by shifting the dissonances from one place to another where the resonance will be most telling. Other chords and arrangements are here indicated: if the first chord is in the lower range, the chord from the opposite series may be placed above in an agreeable dispersion; this is not imperative however, for by adjusting them so as to bring them into direct contact, the piquancy of minor second or the major seventh is emphasized.   A minor second in the upper octave together with a major seventh inversion of the same notes as at Ex. 175 (b) is desirable.   A mixture of sharps and flats facilitates reading.

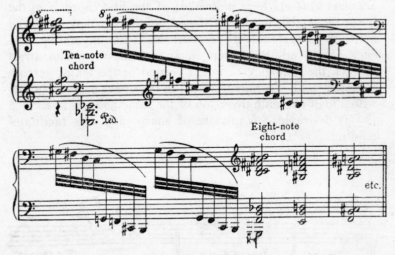

## The Feasibility of Employing This Method of Building For Polytonal Chords

Someone may have observed that, upon first sight, the polytonal chords do not appear to be included in the scheme, and may have reasoned that chord building by fifths and by fourths does not fit into or adapt itself to this whole-tone method in which we build semitonal harmony. This is not the case however, for, in fact, it does this very thing. If we

**Ex. 175** (d) "Elegia Eroica"                    ALFREDO CASELLA

**Ex. 175 (e)**

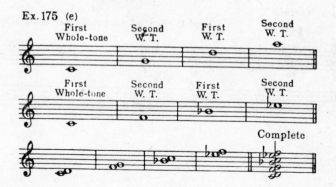

build by fifths, Ex. 175 (e), every alternate note belongs to the adjoining whole-tone scale. So when we analyze the excerpt from Casella's *Elegia Eroica*, Ex. 175 (d), in which he employs the fifth-construction, we find that it fits into the process very well.

If fifths are arranged from alternate whole-tone chord members, fourths so arranged will be found equally satisfactory, because they are inversions of fifths. Ex. 175 (e).

This, however, will not preclude the possibility of still considering the structure, as shown in Ex. 175 (d), a series of superimposed keys; the result nevertheless is semitonal harmony.

The chords in Ex. 175 (f) by Honegger, Stravinsky, Ornstein, Berners, and Varèse might be a part of this process because they are not key-defining.

**Ex. 175 (f)**

Honegger's "Pacific 231"   Stravinsky's "Suite"   Ornstein's "The Corpse"

Varèse's "Octandre"

Lord Berners' "Trois petites marches funèbres."

## Chapter XVII

# CHORD BUILDING BY FOURTHS

## Two, Three, and Four-Note Chords

Chord building by fourths is a subject concerning which very few people have information, yet many are curious to acquire some knowledge of this unexplored field. It has been thought that a few suggestions might be of assistance to those who are, or may become, interested in this most fascinating subject.

Probably the greatest authority on chord building by fourths is Arnold Schönberg in whose book, *Harmonielehre* (Universal Edition), much illuminating information is given.

While most of these combinations, i.e., unresolved appoggiaturas, passing-notes, and elevenths and thirteenths, can be explained along the old lines, their constant use is giving them an identity of their own, and a study of these harmonies of superimposed fourths has become a necessity.

There is a certain feeling of triteness at the present time in using old harmony, and the two old scales are worn threadbare by constant usage. These fourth-built chords, together with the whole-tone harmony, assist in making the tonality vague, a very much desired condition in present-day composition.

Schönberg thinks there is a gap in the method of construction by thirds, and he contends that this process of building by fourths complements the old system. He attempts to expose the theory of extraneous chords as being a badly disguised attempt to fill up the hole with a quantity of waste material and notes foreign to the harmony. To quote: "The number of these unnecessary notes is so great that neither the gap in the harmony, nor even the entire system itself is big enough to hold it . . . . The method of building up chords in fourths is identical with that of fifths and possibly appeals as strongly to the musical ear; it is certainly capable of conducting uniformly all manner of chords with greater surety than by the system of thirds." Further on he says, "I confine myself to giving my reason for discussing chords in fourths, which is that they are justified by the source from which they are derived . . . . So far as I know, the first time I wrote them was in my symphonic poem *Pelléas and Mélisande*. These chords form an isolated instance of the expression of one certain mood, the peculiarity of which forced me, against my will, to invent a new means of expression. Even to this day, I remember having written them with hesitance, but was compelled to do so by their inevitableness.

"A long time afterwards I again used *chords-in-fourths* in my *Chamber Symphony*, without remembering that they had occurred to me before . . . . Here the fourths form an entirely different means of expression, i.e., wild jubilation, in a theme given to the horns."

Ex.176

However this may be, it is undoubtedly true that a mixture of these intervals is one of the most valuable trends of this movement. Note how the chords in Ex. 176, with intervals of fourths in vertical succession between the upper voices and thirds below, give a most satisfactory arrangement; and by the addition of a third above this, a still more valued series results.

These open fourths are more often in the upper parts, but they are sometimes placed below. Note Cyril Scott's *Arabesque*, Ex. 190.

Scriabine's so-called "Mystic Chord" is a combination of

the whole-tone dominant and three *fourths;* all but one note in the series belongs to the whole-tone harmonies.  Most of the nations outside of England do not recognize the eleventh and thirteenth as legitimate chord intervals; they are inclined to call the $f^\sharp$ the lowered fifth, $g^b$, thus eliminating one of the fourths (See Ex. 177).

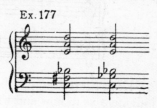

Ex. 177

While the eleventh-and-thirteenth method is a satisfactory way to explain the dominant harmony, it cannot explain the harmony so satisfactorily when it is tonic, so one is led to believe that there is room for the two systems (i.e., thirds and fourths).

Numerous excerpts from various modern composers are shown to illustrate the varied uses of these fourth chords.

Young composers who wish to try some of the newer harmony may begin by an occasional use of these chords as illustrated in the following example showing the harmonization of the old familiar folk-song.  Use a fourth-chord after preparation in soprano.

Ex. 178

The author is not necessarily recommending a process of corrupting our folk-songs; yet, for the theorist and composer, it is astonishing what colorful lines can be evolved.

Note the chords at A, built by perfect fourths, and the whole-tone chord at B in Ex. 179, showing a chord with six different notes, and two duplicates.

Ex. 179

Karg-Elert seems to possess an unusually discriminating judgment as to how and when to use these harmonies. In his "Adeste Fideles" from *Cathedral Windows*, Ex. 180, he employs five-note fourth harmony in the third measure, also in the first two measures in broken chords. *It cannot be emphasized too strongly that one must use the utmost discretion in devising proper ways of handling these harmonies, otherwise they will become a harmonic device not to be desired.* A number of composers have made questionable use of them, and that kind of procedure will have a tendency to prejudice musicians against them (See Ex. 252).

Ex. 180  Adeste Fideles                SIGFRID KARG-ELERT, Op. 106, № 4

### THE TWO-NOTE CHORDS

Naturally the beginnings of writing in fourths were in the early, crude attempts at combining voices, known as diaphony or organum. While these early efforts were later abandoned for the more consonant intervals, the movement in writing at the present time seems to be a reversion to such methods. Just as we go back to the folk-songs of primitive man to extract something that may be of importance which has been overlooked in our refining, civilizing **processes, so** we look to the early attempts at combining voices, hoping to find suggestive material. To Hucbald, a monk of St. Amand in Flanders, is usually ascribed the honor of having first combined voices in this way, and he was wise enough to foresee something of its harmonic possibilities.

As we look at it in the perspective of centuries, that type of harmony, in its quaint crudeness, would seem to be singularly appropriate for that period. We are able to get a proper impression of the times and people in their upward strivings. This diaphonic method is now applied to certain modern harmonic methods described in *A Dictionary of Modern Music and Musicians*, J. M. Dent & Sons, London.

These same fourths are serving composers well in depicting certain grotesque situations, e.g., in Elgar's *Demoniacal Chorus* in *The Dream of Gerontius*.

The addition of another fourth to the two-note chord has brought about a decided transformation. A desire for more direct access to vital upper partials seems to be at the root of the matter. The crudeness largely disappears, and the chords take on a chameleon-like character. If we think of, or play, these chords in terms of the celesta, harp, glockenspiel, upper parts of the piano range and harmonics from the strings, we will arrive at a better understanding of their usefulness (See excerpt from Cyril Scott's Concerto for Piano, Ex. 195).

*The author believes that the future harmony must be thought of in connection with the medium which is to perform it.* This is most decidedly true of the music of Stravinsky— a composer who possesses an almost uncanny sense for the appropriate orchestration of exotic harmony.

## THE THREE-NOTE FOURTH CHORDS

These three-note chords are rapidly coming into common use in present-day composition. They are particularly effective when they are accompanied by an arpeggio-like pro gression in the lower parts, with the upper parts moving diatonically, or by leaps of thirds or fourths.

The example most frequently quoted is from Cyril Scott's *Poème* (Ex. 181).

Ex. 181

In Examples 182 to 190 inclusive we notice the diverse ways in which the composers of the present time are applying this manner of construction. In most temporary works, its use is apparent in more or less disguised forms, not only in three parts but with more voices, forms which will be explained in later chapters.

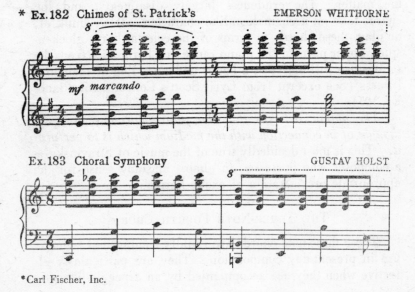

* Ex. 182  Chimes of St. Patrick's    EMERSON WHITHORNE

*mf marcando*

Ex. 183  Choral Symphony    GUSTAV HOLST

*Carl Fischer, Inc.

DEBUSSY

Ex. 184

Ex. 185  Sunset *

KARG-ELERT, Op. 108, №1

Ex. 186  Violin Sonata, №3

HERBERT HOWELLS

etc

*Arthur P. Schmidt Co.

Ex.187  Psychologiques

Lord BERNERS

Ex 188

Song by ARNOLD BAX

An' ye sae douce, ye sneer at this, Ye're

naught but sense - less ass-es Ol

The same

Ex. 189  1922 Suite for Piano "Ragtime"    PAUL HINDEMITH

Ex. 190 Arabesque      CYRIL SCOTT

## Possible Reasons for the Use of Three-Note Fourth Chords

It is interesting to conjecture as to the possible reasons for their use. There are several contributing factors:

1. The introduction of dominant ninths, elevenths and thirteenths.
2. The added-note theory.
3. The unresolved suspensions.
4. Atonalism.
5. A desire for revitalized harmony.

These may be discussed as follows:

1. The construction of chords up to and including the dominant ninth left little opportunity for the use of chord building by fourths. When we speak of fourths, we mean the presence of two or more superimposed fourths. Naturally one fourth has always been present between the fifth and the root, if the fifth is below the root. Ex. 191 (a).

In order to secure two perfect fourths from the dominant, the ninth should be present, so we found the chord occasionally in this position, root in soprano. Ex. 191 (b).

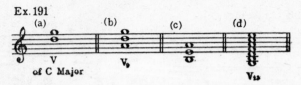

Ex. 191

(a)      (b)      (c)      (d)

V          V₉                    V₁₃

of C Major

The chord shown at Ex. 191 (c) cannot be included in the dominant of the key of *C major* without recognizing the thirteenth as a chord member, Ex. 191 (d). So likewise, the following, Ex. 192 (a), could not be produced without the eleventh.

Ex. 192

(a)                    (b)

V

The chord at Ex. 192 (b) may also be included, but it may be analyzed otherwise.

**Ex. 193**

If we begin by building down in fourths from the seventh of the dominant thirteenth, we secure the following chord of seven notes with the root a third below the last one of them:

While this is usually impracticable as a chord unit, it may be divided in the following way:

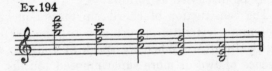

Ex. 194

Any one of these triads of fourths may well represent the dominant harmony if the root is present in the bass. This should explain the numerous fourth-chords that so frequently appear as substitutes for the plain triad or dominant seventh.

The following excerpt from Cyril Scott's Piano Concerto

gives one a vivid illustration of this use of dominant eleventh and thirteenth harmony. Here the celesta above, and the harp below, together with other subdued, sustained parts lend it a glamour which is fascinating.

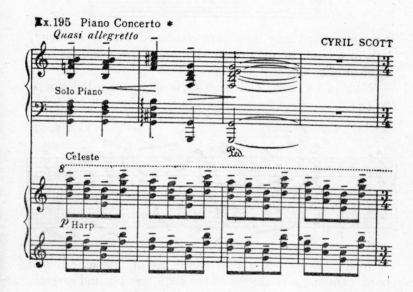

Ex. 195  Piano Concerto *

*Quasi allegretto*

CYRIL SCOTT

Solo Piano

Celeste

*p* Harp

2. In order to have the tonic chord clothed in appropriate garb to agree with the dominant chord, notes were added to it, because of the inappropriateness of the tonic thirteenth as a usable chord.

By adding a second to the tonic, we are enabled to arrange our tonic chord with two fourths, Ex. 196 (a), and by the addition of the sixth, we have the result shown at Ex. 196 (b), which with the third makes four fourths; with the addition of major seventh to tonic, we secure a six-tone chord Ex. 196 (c).

*Schott & Co., Ltd.

Ex.196
(a)    (b)    (c)

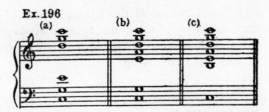

The tonic chord may then have combined with it a second, sixth, or seventh, or any two, or all three of these, and the feeling of finality will still be retained.

Note in Ex. 197 Cyril Scott's use of the chord shown at 196 (b).

Ex.197   Diatonic Study                           CYRIL SCOTT

In Ex. 198 we find a most clever use of this tonic fourth chord, bringing into use the added sixth, second, and seventh, so arranged as to display the use of fourths in an attractive manner. (See last two measures. Also last five measures of Eugène Goossens' *Nature Poem*, No. 3, not quoted.)

MARIO CASTELNUOVO-TEDESCO

Ex.198   Il Passo delle Nazarene

Still another illustration of this method of construction is shown in Ex. 199.   As a rule Scriabine employs a different method of building, but it coincides very nearly with that illustrated in the other quotations (see Ex. 263).

Ex. 199  Vers la flamme, Op. 72 *                     SCRIABINE

3.   At the present time we frequently find the evasion of the resolution of the suspension, the third in particular.   Any of the devices of the older school are studiously avoided in an endeavor to introduce novel features into compositions, so we find instead of the arrangement as shown in Ex. 200 (a) and (c), where the suspensions resolve, that the note suspending the third remains stationary as at Ex. 200 (b) and (d).

*Chord with sixth, major seventh, and augmented eleventh added to tonic.

In one sense we substitute the eleventh for the third (Ex. 274). In Holst's Planets (Ex. 292), we find the melody moving along these lines.

4. When three voices only are present, and arranged in fourths, we are not sure to what key the chord belongs, and later, as we add other fourths to the chord, it becomes more and more ambiguous. Take for example the following three-tone triad of fourths with

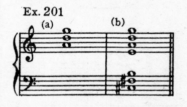

added notes in the second measure. To this one chord of three voices arranged by superimposed fourths, one may add a considerable variety of notes above and below. All the resulting chords are somewhat indefinite as to tonality.

These chords, therefore, are a valuable aid to present-day composition where a certain amount of vagueness is desirable. If one wishes, they may easily be adapted to some one tonality by applying a dominant bass; and it seems wise at present thus to associate them with some definite key.

5. The innovation thus far described gave new vitality to the old chords. This may have been a somewhat uncon-

scious movement, but experimentation brought other results such as the following: by using the dominant chord with lowered fifth and raised fifth, and writing the latter as the minor thirteenth ($e^b$, in the key of $C$, instead of a $d^\sharp$) together with a minor ninth, we obtain the very interesting chords with two perfect fourths shown at (a) and (b), in Ex. 202.

**Ex. 202**

Again, as a possible experiment, by lowering the third of the dominant, two more tones may be added to the perfect-fourth series, and we have a set of five tones by fourths. See Ex. 203 (a).

In Ex. 203 and 204 are shown some of the methods of present-day composers. The dominants are undergoing transformations.

**Ex. 203 Kammersymphonie**      A. SCHÖNBERG

**Ex. 204 Short Sonata**      YORK BOWEN

## Further Developments of Dominant Harmony

In Ex. 207 are appended various chord substitutes for traditional dominant harmony. All one needs to do is to choose a ground note and build on it. Almost any combination of fourths will unite to make a dominant, especially in the upper three or four voices; other parts may sometimes supply a seventh, a third, or a fifth. Resolutions of these chords to the tonic, similarly arranged, are also possible, at least for those chords which include an added sixth, second, or seventh, or any two, or all three of these.

When we use these combinations, we are naturally eliding the resolution of certain parts of the chord; e.g., the natural resolution of the following chord is as illustrated:

Ex. 205

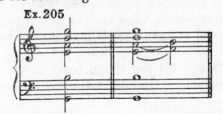

All the chords shown in Ex. 207 may be accounted for as implying resolutions with which our ears can now willingly dispense. This process of elision is not new. Every harmony text-book suggests places where this evolution has taken place. Ex. 206 is a case in point.

Ex. 206

Dr. George Dyson in his book *The New Music*, Oxford University Press, in speaking of unresolved notes, says, "It is possible to 'hear' this imaginary resolution, just as in moments of strained attention one can 'hear' a pianissimo note on a violin for some time after the bow has ceased to touch the string. But with increasing familiarity, the ear begins to dispense with such inferences." Ex. 207.

## The Four-Note Fourth Chords

The four-note fourth chords may be used impressionistically, that is, by the parallel movement of all parts, either chromatically or diatonically, ascending or descending. Just

Ex. 207

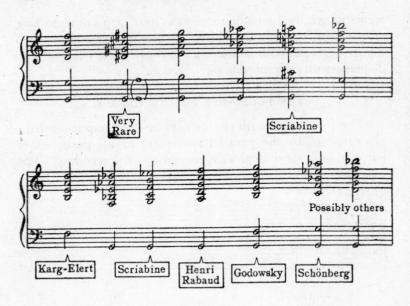

as fundamental sevenths may be written with similar motion of all parts, so these chords may be employed, with results of a somewhat corresponding utility.

Ex. 208

Note Honegger's use of the above device, in Ex. 216.

The next example shows how effectively such chord progressions may be used to imitate chimes.

**Ex. 209**

In our traditional system of harmony these fourth-combinations appeared occasionally in the following way, not as real chords, but as incidental harmonies:

**Ex. 210**

This combination of fourths appeared in place of the dominant six-four-three chord, and was analyzed as an organ-point in the alto and tenor, or as an unresolved suspension in the alto; or as produced by passing-notes in the bass and soprano.

If one desires to use these combinations as chords, it can be accomplished easily in an impressionistic way. By resolving the suspension to the third of the chord at any time desired, it becomes a dominant in its second inversion. Ex. 211 (a). Still another analysis of this chord might be to call it the dominant eleventh with the third omitted (the eleventh substitutes for the third). A modern resolution of the chord could be as shown in Ex. 211 (b). See also Ex. 212.

The possibility of using these new combinations as chords, incidental harmonies, between our old chords, i.e., chromatically inserted as shown at A in Ex. 212, with four voices, and also with five, six and seven parts, as shown at A in Ex. 213, is worth considering.

Karg-Elert frequently resolves his fourth chords as shown in the last two measures, i.e., to a triad with the third in the bass (see Ex. 217). This gives an effective means of employing the chromatic notes more fully. Note particularly (c) in Ex. 213 where all five voices move chromatically to and from the chord, an impossible situation with our harmony up to the present time. One hardly realizes that a harsh discord is being played, it is so smoothly introduced. Other examples of a similar kind are shown at A in Ex. 213 (e), (g), (i), and (k).

**Ex. 213**

If the upper tones are resolved one half-step down, the arrangement is better, and a sequence might be carried out in this way:

**Ex. 214**

One advantage in the use of these chords is their ambiguity of key. They can resolve to many keys with equal facility.

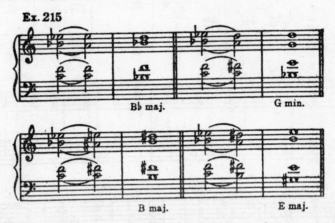

In the Honegger excerpt for orchestra, we have an ingenious use of fourth chords in rapid scales played by the strings. Later in the work, Ex. 216, the celesta takes over these chords, imparting to them a touch of exquisite delicacy.

*Maurice Senart.

The next example is from a composition for organ.

Ex. 217  Landscape in Mist

SIGFRID KARG-ELERT, Op.96, №2

*Quieto e indeciso*

## Chapter XVIII

# CHORD BUILDING BY FOURTHS

## (*Continued*)

### The Five and Six-Note Chords

The five-note chords may be used impressionistically, but necessarily they are more dissonant than the chords previously considered, and therefore less workable; and yet, if ingeniously placed, they exceed in value the chords of fewer tones. They are particularly useful if resolved to chords of the old system, or to the new whole-tone dominant.

Most of these chords necessitate chromatic alterations in some of the factors. There are three in major keys, however, that do not require such changes outside the regular signature. Most of the examples are worked in the key of *C major* (see Ex. 230 and 231 for solutions in the minor) for ease in analysis.

Ex. 218

III⁴      VI⁴      VII⁴

All but one of the following have unaltered soprano notes; one, two, three, and four respectively, of the lower notes are raised:

**Ex. 219**

Other possible combinations are shown below (with altered upper notes):

**Ex. 220**

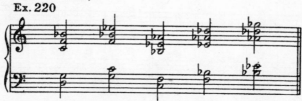

Strange though it may seem at first to construct on definite scale steps these unusual combinations, it is a process in actual use in present-day composition. See Schönberg's use of what is apparently a II₄ chord of five voices (Ex. 239).

The chords of approach and resolution for some of these fourth combinations will now be shown: The III₄ chord:

**Ex. 221**

Cyril Scott employs this III₄ chord in four parts in the following example:

**Ex. 222** Old World Minuet

CYRIL SCOTT

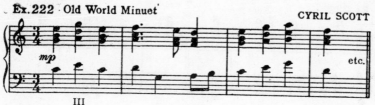

**Ex. 223** The VI Chord

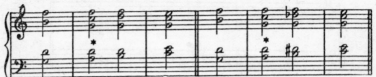

**Ex. 224**

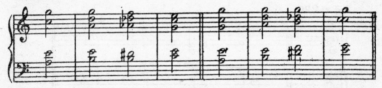

The III₄ chord might take the place of the tonic $^6_4$ or II₇ at the cadence.

**Ex. 225**

III₄　V₇　　I　　　　I$^6_4$　II₇　V₇

Resolution of the IV with **raised root**:

**Ex. 226**

Resolution of the I with two lower notes raised:

Resolutions of the remaining chords shown in Ex. 219:

A chord with altered note in highest voice (from Ex. 220):

Some of the chords with their upper note lowered work well in the minor key:

The next two examples illustrate, respectively progressions by thirds and fourths in downward motion:

In Chapter XVII, where a detailed description of the dominant chord with raised and lowered fifth occurred (Ex. 202), we notice that if the *b* in the tenor of Ex. 202 (b) is lowered, we have the five-note perfect-fourth chord as explained in this chapter. Compare Ex. 233 (a) and (b). So we can see how closely allied these fourth chords may be to the dominant of some key.

Resolutions of other familiar chords are shown at (c) in Ex. 233.

Ex. 233

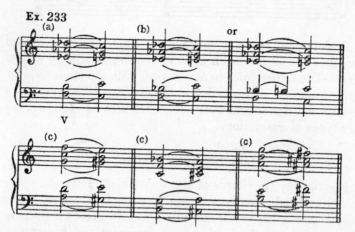

If, however, these represent dominant 4-2 chords, the root of the chord may be added a minor seventh below in the bass, thus making a five-note fourth chord with added bass, Ex. 234 (a), (b), and (c).

Ex. 234

Speaking of the tyranny of the dominant, here is another way to gain freedom; in Holst's *Choral Symphony*, observe how the chords seem to take this form:

Ex. 235  Choral Symphony  GUSTAV HOLST

A dominant in some guise must exist, and this second chord has the signification of one, coming as it does at this point. The upper voice here cadences with the modal whole-step. Attention is also called to the fact that Holst resolves a five-tone chord to a four-tone one. See also Ex. 241 (a), for other types of resolution.

### THE SIX-NOTE CHORD

Has the day for chords of six, seven, eight and more notes arrived? Traditionally, the chord has been regarded, in the main, as consisting of not more than five different notes, as in the case of the ninth chords of the dominant and supertonic. All other notes could be analyzed as suspensions or appoggiaturas. The whole-tone dominant with its six different tones and the fourth chords with their six different tones or more, presage a new era in our musical development.

Ex. 236

If we build chords by fourths, the parts may multiply to the number of twelve. This includes all notes in the chromatic scale, a number which Schönberg claims he and his pupils have written. See also the example by Jean Huré in Lenormand's *Modern Harmony*, page 127, and Casella's *Notte de Maggio*. These twelve-note chords are rather formidable, but those with six, seven, and eight notes are not disagreeable if properly introduced and resolved.

Up to the present point in this book, the fourth chords have been resolved mainly to chords of our old harmonic system. But they seem to demand those of a different type, something that does not rest on our ears too lightly. Nevertheless—and especially when six or more voices are used—the degree of dissonance should gradually reduce in resolutions, as when we use II₇-V₇-I. Consequently these six-note fourth chords resolve well to the six-note whole-tone dominant, a chord not quite so dissonant. A remarkable continuous six-voice sequence may be constructed in this way; it is entirely different from those to which we are accustomed. Ex. 237 shows this, with six voices at (a) and (b) and with eight voices at (c).

The number of valuable sequences that can be founded on these progressions will be obvious to any well-trained musician. In Ex. 238 are shown two whole-tone dominant resolutions, each fourth-chord resolving in two different ways.

Such chords destroy the key feeling and are therefore useful in the newer school of composition where it is desirable to avoid any one tonality. The bass note may become the root of the dominant, however, and resolve accordingly.

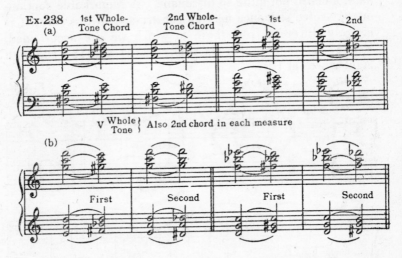

Schönberg here resolves to the dominant seventh and dominant ninth only.

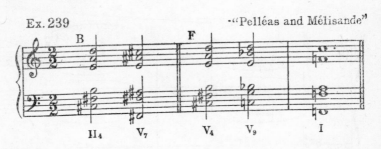

Ex. 239 — "Pelléas and Mélisande"

Ex. 240 is an extract illustrating the use of these chords and others, showing how they may be utilized in our modern technic.

Ex. 240   Piano Sonata                                    H. A. M.

The following example shows a few peculiar resolutions of these fourth chords. These strange new harmonies require various sorts of odd successions that will be somewhat in keeping with their exotic character. At (b) the six-tone chords progress in contrary motion toward each other and to the same fourth chord; at (c) and (d) directly to the tonic; and at (f) the upper parts act as a compound organ-point with interpolations.

Ex.241

Ex. 242 illustrates the use of various fourth chords in parallel motion of all parts, but in (a), (b), and (c) one of the fourths is omitted; in (d) the two lower parts double two of the upper parts, while in (e) there is an arrangement whereby the two sets of parts move in contrary motion. These may be taken in all kinds of tempos, employing, if for orchestra, some of the new color schemes appropriate for such harmony.   (See also Chapter XIX, where more parts are similarly used.)

Ex 242

In Ex. 243 Lord Berners uses these fourth chords in the manner shown at (a) in Ex. 242.

Ex. 243   Fragments psychologiques
*Allegro*                                      Lord BERNERS

In Ex. 244 and 245 are suggested ways of vitalizing our harmonies.

Ex. 244   For Piano                                      H. A. M.

Ex. 245   Piano Sonata                                   H. A. M.

Exs. 246, 247 and 248 show various uses of six-note and other fourth chords.

Ex. 246  Sonata

*Allegro*

DARIUS MILHAUD

Ex. 247  Feuille d'album, Nº 1

*Andante sostenuto*

RÉBIKOFF

etc.

ALFREDO CASELLA

Ex. 248  Antigrazioso

It is evident that if harmony is to be rescued from its monotony, new methods of construction must be employed. Our best and newest chords at the present time are impossible of analysis along the old lines. Composers of any importance must have new problems to solve; it is preposterous that they should be expected to work in the old way.

A glimpse into the hitherto unsuspected scope of this new harmonic material can be gained by a study of the following

Ex.249(a) Chamber Symphony, Op. 9                    SCHÖNBERG

extracts from Schönberg's *Chamber Symphony*. For several measures, Ex. 249, he uses this material in shifting arpeggios, later employing harmonics (flageolet tones) in 'cello and viola;

Ex. 249 (b)

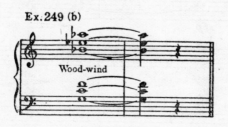

also it enters into Ex. 250 and 251—in the latter example this harmony is introduced in the fashion of an appoggiatura chord, finally resolving pleasantly in agreeable, unexpected ways to consonance.

Ex. 250 Kammersymphonie                    SCHÖNBERG, Op. 9
1st Violin

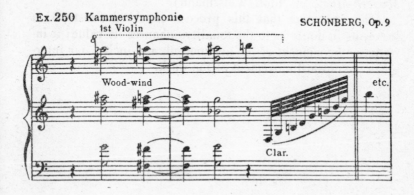

The pizzicato strings accompanied by sustained wood-winds later resolve into a muted major chord.

Ex. 251

Devices to soften the natural harshness of some such combinations should be applied. We may not accept all of Schönberg's ideas as employed in composition, but it is certain that he can teach us many rare and useful things, if we are unprejudiced. "His opinion is worth the attention of those who are far from being Schönbergians" (*Problems of Modern Music* by Adolf Weissmann).

The very fact that this process of chord construction leaves us in doubt as to the tonality enhances its value; it introduces the element of the unexpected, and incites our interest in the onward movement of the work.

## Chapter XIX

## CHORD BUILDING BY FOURTHS
### (*Continued*)

### Chords of Seven, Eight, and More Notes

When we multiply parts, the difficulty of handling these chords is increased, but it is amazing how well they sound, considering the number of parts. Note the first measure of Ex. 258, where ten distinct parts with no duplications are present. The examples in contrary-motion are particularly useful. Of course, we are giving the merest harmonic outline. With proper variation of these forms many useful specimens could be secured.

Perhaps such harmony should largely be confined to the piano, with its evanescent qualities in which the harshness becomes dissipated, evaporated.

Ex. 252  Feuille d'album, №1        V. REBIKOFF
*Andante sostenuto*

Ex. 252 shows Rebikoff's use of seven-note, and Ex. 259, eight-note chords. It is a very easy task to write such harmony and therefore not always the most satisfying in the result. A certain amount of contrary motion, as shown in Ex. 256, 257, and 258 adds interest; an alternation of fourth-chord harmony with whole-tone chords, as shown in Ex. 254

and in the quotation (Ex. 260) from the piano solo, can give the desired variety.

Gustav Holst also makes use of seven and eight-note fourth chords, including some of mixed constitution in the *Evening Watch*, probably written at about the same time as his *Choral Symphony*. (See Ex. 255.)

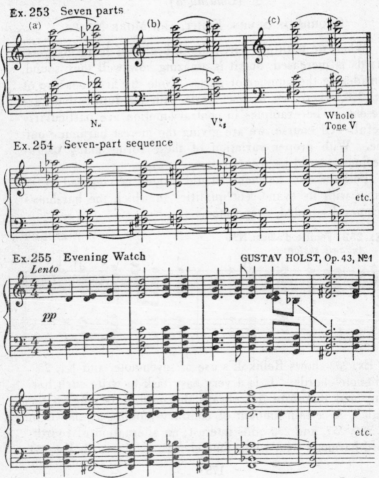

Ex. 253 Seven parts

(a)    (b)    (c)

N₇        V⁹₇        Whole Tone V

Ex. 254 Seven-part sequence

etc.

Ex. 255 Evening Watch        GUSTAV HOLST, Op. 43, №1

Lento

pp

etc.

**Ex. 256. Seven parts** (Diminishing to six)

**Ex. 257  Nine parts** (Diminishing to seven)

**Ex. 258  Ten parts** (Diminishing to eight)

**Ex. 259 · Feuille d'album, № 1**

*Andante sostenuto*  (Eight parts)  V. RÉBIKOFF

etc.

Ex. 260  Chameleonesque

*Allegretto*

H. A. M.

Should one wish to employ all the seven parts of a dominant thirteenth chord arranged by perfect fourths only, he should build down from the seventh or up from the third. The interval of a third will be the only interval appearing outside of the fourth, and this occurs between root and third. If one builds otherwise, the augmented fourth will occur between the seventh and third. Naturally this is not a crime, but is simply a suggestion of the old school.

Ex. 261

$V_{13}$

3rd of V

etc.

A break in the diatonic series begins when the series of fourths is continued below the third of v.

This then is the unaltered thirteenth with all parts present, arranged by perfect fourths. One may use a number of combinations from this chord alone. So it is apparent that the dominant can be represented in numerous forms. This should explain the many groupings of fourths that are used in connection with the dominant. Seven different soprano notes from this chord alone may be employed. We are now making use of the diatonic notes only. In Ex. 261 a few of the possible combinations are given. The chord may also be arranged as suggested in Chapter xx and still represent dominant harmony (see Ex. 195).

With the augmented fourth present, the chords take on the following appearance:

Ex. 262

These forms are not so adaptable as the former ones, and this is probably the reason Scriabine altered the elevenths; for instance, in Ex. 263, *c* to *c*♯.

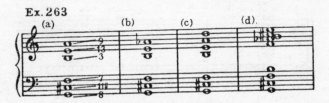

Ex. 263

This gives him the augmented fourth, the diminished fourth, another augmented fourth, and two perfect fourths. See page 12 of his Sonata No. 5. In his Sonata No. 7 he alters the ninth to a minor ninth, Ex. 263 (b) and in *Prometheus* the fifth is added, Ex. 263 (c). Scriabine's methods were quite different from those of all previous composers. He chose chords from the harmonic series and exploited them, evolving the whole composition out of one or two harmonies. He adopts these chords as perfect concords and one is expected to accept them as such with all their inversions; so we find this strange combination in *Prometheus*:

Ex. 264 **Prometheus**

The fourths appear frequently in such chords; even the whole-tone chord may be so arranged:

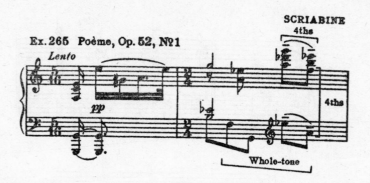

Ex. 265 Poème, Op. 52, №1

One can readily distinguish between Schönberg's and Scriabine's fourth chords by noting whether or not an altered fourth is used; the augmented eleventh is invariably present in the works of Scriabine, and usually in a lower part. Perhaps these alterations are an advantage, but the fourths are frequently visual only. Most of Schönberg's fourths are perfect, in sound and notation. In some ways this type of chord seems coldly calculating, but if we analyze the following chords there can certainly be no doubt of their practicability.

Ex. 266

If again we take the series shown in Ex. 261, using six of the upper notes of the dominant thirteenth, the number of bass notes that may be used to supplement the chord is astonishing.

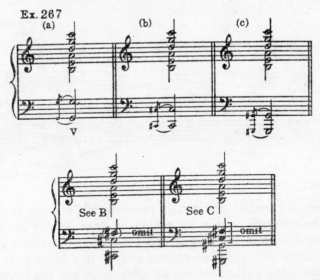

In Ex. 267, at (a), we have the dominant thirteenth; at (b), the $c^\sharp$ is a bass note two fourths below the $b$ and belonging to the series of fourths; at (c) the $g^\sharp$ is the next fourth below the $c^\sharp$. The spacing allows this. Other fourths below are a possibility until one in the series is employed.

The resolution of these chords is a difficult task. A simple tonic is not at all appropriate, nor any plain triad, nor

**Ex. 268  Seven-part sequence**

even the dominant seventh. Very strong dissonances are required. In the sequences built up in the following examples, we find at last appropriate places to use the dominant elevenths and thirteenths. In Ex. 268, the first chord of each pair is a fourth chord; alternate chords are dominant elevenths.

In Ex. 269 the alternate chords are dominant elevenths and thirteenths.

Ex. 269

In Ex. 270 the alternate chords are whole-tone dominants.

Ex. 270

# CHAPTER XX

## OTHER WAYS OF COMBINING FOURTH CHORDS

If with the three-tone fourth chord we combine another two or three-tone chord not a perfect fourth below, but a downward major third, we acquire a new and favorite combination. Cyril Scott,* Karg-Elert, and Gustav Holst have used this procedure very often.

Ex. 271 Choral Symphony — GUSTAV HOLST

And each vi - brates the string

Ex. 272 Choral Symphony — GUSTAV HOLST

Ex. 273 Angelus — CYRIL SCOTT

etc.

*See excerpt from Piano Concerto (Ex. 195).

184

The lute, which flourished in the seventeenth century, at one time had a similar tuning, i.e., with six strings, three above and three below, in fourths, the two sets placed a major third apart. Ex. 274 (a). One can imagine these six strings being sounded together in a higher stopping with much the same effect as that which is now obtained when the chord at (b) is played *8va* on the modern pianoforte.

*Ex. 274
(a)                                                                    (b)*

V Lute Dominant

This method of writing probably derived its origin from the fact that any secondary seventh chord with the seventh in the bass shows the two fourths a major third apart (Ex. 275).

**Ex. 275**

This combination was used impressionistically, and later a desire for fuller harmony influenced writers to add fourths below and above, sometimes to the upper part and other times below, causing the major third to shift from one part of the chord to another. This manner of writing is much used by Karg-Elert, and it seems to be a most satisfactory way. Note Ex. 276, from an organ number by this composer, in *Cathedral Windows*.

*This "lute dominant" is used by Godowsky in his Java Suite, Book III, No. 7.

**Ex. 276** Lauda Sion
from "Cathedral Windows"    SIGFRID KARG-ELERT

*ff fastoso e grandioso*    *p mistico*

This shifting, combined with an occasional complete perfect fourth chord of five or six parts, lends itself to a satisfying effect. Perfect fourth chords are somewhat artificial in their make-up and an exchange of interval tends to relieve the monotony. This method of building has a real harmonic value, and it can easily be added to our old system.

Many composers are using fourth chords with unattractive results. It is rather absurd to mechanicalize a valuable trend in musical composition by a reckless use of fourths such as Rebikoff's in *Feuille d'Album*, already quoted.

It is not necessary that the intervals of fourth chords with a major third introduced shall always be dispersed in the way illustrated thus far. If the lower combination is placed an octave higher, or the upper an octave lower, we interlock the two sets, so to speak, and the result gives us three pairs of major seconds.* This is another process that is much used (Ex. 277). The seconds all being major, their harshness is negligible.

**Ex. 277**

Maj. third    Transposed

*See footnote page 188.

In the Holst excerpts, Ex. 278 (a) and (b), and the Malipiero *Pause del Silenzio*, Ex. 279, this process is convincingly shown.

Ex. 278 (a) Choral Symphony     (b)     HOLST

Ex. 279   Pause del Silenzio     MALIPIERO

Having arrived at this point, we may observe that the notes of one of the five-tone scales appear (resultant chord in Ex. 278 (a) appears in Ex. 280, third scale, in enharmonic form).

Helmholtz in his *Sensations of Tone* says about five-tone scales: "The intervals between the tones which make up the scales are the same as the intervals between the black keys on the piano." If we accept the added-note theory explained in Chapter XVII, Page 145, all the notes of any of the five-tone scales may be combined to make a chord. To anyone who has attempted to harmonize a pentatonic melody, this tendency is no doubt evident. It will be recalled that a similar process is used in whole-tone harmony, Chapter XIV.

In Charles T. Griffes' harmonization of ancient Chinese and Japanese melodies, this tendency to combine pentatonic

scale notes is noticeable. See Ex. 281 and 282. As said
before, such combinations may be explained on the basis of
unresolved appoggiaturas, or as principal notes and appogia-
turas sounding at the same time.

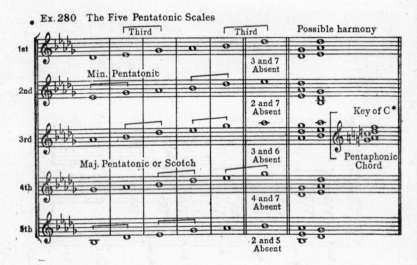

Ex. 280   The Five Pentatonic Scales

Ex. 281   Japanese (13th Century)        CHARLES T GRIFFES, Op. 10, № 2
*Dolente*

One of the peculiar difficulties in writing music of this
type is the securing of proper bass notes.   With reference to
the common three-note fourth chord, good practice seems to
indicate, in the first place, their use over a pedal.   See Chapter XVII, Ex. 184 and 185.   In the excerpt from the organ
piece quoted herewith, where more voices are used over a

*Alfredo Casella, in his book *The Evolution of Music*, describes the chord used
by Debussy in his *Cathedrale engloutie* as a pentaphonic chord (the five notes
being those of the Chinese scale) which substitutes for the dominant.

double pedal-point, the final tonic chord containing the added sixth, second, and seventh will be found a most agreeable arrangement. See Ex. 284.

This is only another proof that the added-note theory is in part responsible for construction by fourths—observe that if we omit the upper *g* in the final chord, the next four notes

Ex. 282  T'ang Dynasty (905-618) B.C.

CHARLES T. GRIFFES

And thick dust o- -ver-spreads the

'broid-ered stoles.

etc.

Ex. 283 (a) Chinese Theme

H. A. M

*p*

etc.

Ex. 283 (b)                                                    H. A. M.

Ex. 284  Seven Pastels, Op. 96, No. 1          SIGFRID KARG-ELERT

below form a chord in fourths. An ending of this kind
makes an appeal to one's aesthetic sense.

The second way to secure bass notes might be to supply
other fourths belonging to the series. To quote again from
instances of such combinations in the works of Karg-Elert:

Ex. 285  Seven Pastels, Op. 96, No. 1          SIGFRID **KARG-ELERT**

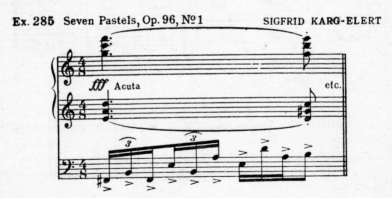

It will be noticed that if the series of fourths were extended downward two more fourths below the manual parts, i.e., to $g^{\#}$, for the first chord, the bass could be easily accounted for; otherwise the task would not be so easy. One can secure a variety of bass notes of the most exotic character by this process of adding under-fourths; a listener realizes at once that the ordinary root, third, fifth, and seventh do not then constitute the series.

If we build these harmonies from a middle point outward, beginning with a major third, it is natural to try other intervals. This has been accomplished by some composers, perhaps more or less unconsciously. Placing the two sets of fourths a fifth apart, we find only a partial duplication in the octave (Ex. 286). The chord sounds well, also, with the inserted interval of a major sixth, as does the same chord inverted (Ex. 287). ·

Ex. 286                                          GUSTAV HOLST

Ex. 287

Fourth chords with inserted major and minor sevenths and augmented fourth are also illustrated, with their resolutions, in Ex. 289, 290 and 291. Many of these new and untried ways of combining tones might be studied with beneficial results. If one can hear mentally the resolution of these new combinations, their harshness at once diminishes. Has not the process been the same in all our aural developments?

Eric Satie uses the augmented fourth separation in his *Fils des étoiles*, placing the interval near the upper part of the chord (Ex. 296). In Lord Berners' *Fragments*, he uses the diminished fifth and augmented fourth at the beginning, and later the augmented fifth (Ex. 295).

If one uses this type of harmony, it is inevitable that sooner or later the notes of the chord will be used in arpeggio form, both in accompaniment figure and in melody, and evidences of this procedure are noticeable in modern composition (see Ex. 288, L. Godowsky, and also Ex. 297).

\* Ex. 288   The Ruined Water Castle at Djokja
            (Java Suite)                    . LEOPOLD GODOWSKY

Note particularly the trumpet parts in Holst's *Planets,* in the fourth part, *Jupiter,* Ex. 292; in Herbert Howells's *Violin and Piano Sonata No. 1* (Ex. 293); also in his *Piano Concerto* (Ex. 294).

\*Carl Fischer, Inc.

Other places where this melodic tendency is noticeable (the parts are not quoted in this book) are in *Le Poème de l'Extase* by Scriabine, *Chamber Symphony* by Schönberg, and in the *Song and Bacchanal*, Holst's Symphony.

Sir Walford Davies in his lecture, *The Perfect Fourth* (from Hucbald to Holst), delivered at Gresham College, and later printed in the *Musical Times,* London, says "May it not be as natural today to move from combined thirds and fifths to combined seconds and fourths as it was a thousand years ago to move from fifths and fourths to the triads themselves?" Be that as it may, it is certain that fourth chords will be one of the "new harmonic devices" of the future composer, not necessarily as a continuous idiom, but as one of the methods of giving new color to worn-out common chords;—this in spite of the strong antagonism from certain well-meaning musicians who are inhospitable toward new processes.

Ex. 289

Ex. 290

Ex. 291

Ex. 292  The Planets                    GUSTAV HOLST, Op. 32

Ex. 293  Sonata for Violin and Piano, Nº 1          HERBERT HOWELLS

Ex. 294  Piano Concerto

HERBERT HOWELLS

*poco allargando*

etc.

Ex. 295  Fragments

Lord BERNERS

Ex. 296  Le Fils des Etoiles

ERIC SATIE

Ex.297   Joseph's Legende                    RICHARD STRAUSS.

## Chapter XXI

## ATONALITY

Polytonality clings tenaciously to the seven-tone scale and common chord, but atonality evades all diatonic methods. This latter is one of the most venturesome of the recent innovations in musical composition.

The diminished seventh chord was the most definite illustration of a possible suggestion of atonality in the old music. This chord, because of being representable enharmonically in several different keys, delegates to itself an indefiniteness of tonality (provided this vagueness is taken advantage of), that is one of the first steps in atonality. It has been peculiarly appropriate in all kinds of dramatic situations, but has lost a large part of this effect by constant use.

As a rule atonal harmony is decidedly exotic, and if one does find traditional harmony it is inclined to have an independent movement. The structure is chromatic and in a way entirely different from that which has been used. The harmony by fourths is one type for such ambiguous modes of speech. Arnold Schönberg is the one artist who is pre-eminently responsible for such methods.

"It must be clear to every intelligent and fair observer that the diatonic system created by the seventeenth century had reached in *Tristan* and through the Romantics the extreme limits of its possibilities, and that the efforts of the post-Wagnerian composers therefore had necessarily to be directed toward a new tonal (or one might say atonal) horizon, polymodal at first (Debussy, Pizzetti, etc.) and chromatic later (Schönberg, etc.)" Alfredo Casella in *The Evolution of Music*.

To quote Edward Burlingame Hill, in his book, *Modern French Music*: "The radical currents of thought in present-day music proceed in two directions—one that of polyharmony with superposed 'harmonic' planes of dissimilar tonalities, the other of 'linear music,' lines of melodic aspect combined in unorthodox counterpoint with atonal relations, that is, conforming to no fixed principle of key relationship."

There are many compositions which are considered atonal, when they should not be so classified. There are certain types of harmony that may be very chromatic, suggesting indefinite tonality, but whose foundation is laid with the diatonic principle in mind; therefore these types cannot be classified as atonal harmony.

The musician of tomorrow will be compelled to discriminate between diatonic chromaticism and atonal chromaticism. The first emphasizes the seven-note scale with the intervening half-steps, and the latter the twelve-note scale and the negation of the triad. Egon Wellesz says in his biography of Schönberg, "In atonal music a system of law obtains, the rules of which for us, who are in the midst of the event, can not yet be formulated."

It is an absolute break with tradition in every respect, and that is always a difficult task even if it is a desirable one. Whether Schönberg's melody and harmony will be fully assimilated in the future is considered doubtful by many leading musicians, but it would seem that a composer of his attainments is worthy of our consideration (see excerpt from song, Ex. 298).

As to the future of music, no one can prophesy; it has changed radically since the sixteenth century, and we may expect a still greater transformation in the next hundred years. At present, it seems by some to remain static; certainly the diatonic type has served its day, and music is in a transitional stage. One can conceive of a type of music outside of previous experience, strange, unearthly and yet music with a certain fascination that will be almost hypnotic in its effect. An occasional glimpse of what future music will possibly be is now and then indicated by certain of our modern composers. Music cannot be expected to be immune from the influence of the exotic. When one considers the emotions engendered by the thrilling experiences of life, and the mystery of the universe in all its obscurity, it is not strange that music should strive to express some of these in a language corresponding to them.

Therefore if the texture of music is unusual and does not meet with our approval, we should not be disconcerted, for it seems that the first step in this new music must be almost revolutionary. A. Eaglefield Hull says in his *Modern Harmony,* "It is only natural that artists should drop the idioms of the great masters as soon as they have become vulgarized by much repetition and base imitation, and in consequence use newer methods of chord-building, progression, and resolution in seeking self-expression."

"If it were desired to outline in a few words the harmonic technique of the last few years, it might be said that it lies in the progressive elimination of the old elementary chords and the more and more searching exploitation of those 'exceptional' chords which have long existed in music in a latent state. At the same time, modulation, which before the nineteenth century was inconceivable otherwise than in succession,

Ex. 298 Der verlorene Haufen          ARNOLD SCHÖNBERG

has been introduced into the simultaneity of a chord the aggregate of which may thus be formed of notes belonging to different keys previously considered mutually incompatible."—Alfredo Casella.

What modern music is and is not, and the nature of its divergence from the old music, are satisfactorily suggested by William Arms Fisher in an article read before the M. T. N. A. in 1923. "Now we are so accustomed to the old scale system that to get away from sense of tonality, of key center, is extremely difficult; the very effort seems unnatural. Yet right here you put your finger on 'modernism.' Your modernist is seeking freedom from the autocracy of a 'tonic center,' and the ultramodernist is seeking to abolish it altogether."

The music of today points to the fact that the absolute reign of diatonic tonality has begun to decline. Just what diatonic tonality is and how long it has taken man to determine its meaning, is one of the interesting items in the evolution of music. Probably the only correct criterion in the formation of a theory in regard to the diatonic principle is the necessary inclusion and co-operation, concurrently, of both the melodic and harmonic elements.

A certain amount of tonal insecurity confronts the modern listener, and yet by this very indefiniteness his attention is held at a high point of expectancy. In this modern product dissonances are used as points of rest, the major seventh being particularly appropriate because of its ambiguity. The dominant seventh, if used with its classical implications, is the one chord that must be eschewed; no chord gives tonality a more determinative fixedness than this binding element in the fabric of classical diatonicism.

If atonalism is employed and the dominant formations (mainly ninths) are to be used, they should be used impressionistically, or at least in some deceptive manner, in order to avoid the inevitable tonic which leads to a definite tonality.

There are probably varying degrees of atonalism, the textures of which may be diversified, but if one is to secure the unusual atonal state employed by Schönberg, dominants of the type mentioned above must be ignored as too obvious an element.

Ralph Waldo Emerson says that a jumble of musical sounds on a viol or flute gives pleasure to the unskillful ear. Perhaps all musicians' ears are arriving at that blissful state, for they seem to be able to assimilate very dissonant chords and derive pleasure from them. One must remember however that a continuous, cacophonic bombardment of our aural perceptions will not bring us eventual elation or satisfaction of a permanent type. These overpungent harmonies should be used intermittently; the contrast of such artifices with less complex mediums will give better results.

That the theorists are showing an increasing sign of erudition is well indicated by George W. Gow in his article, *Theory*, read before the M. T. N. A., 1926, in which he says, after observing the number of theory books by recent composers, "There is vitality in present methods, and an eager look to the future. Since the modern text-book is the composer's page, and the slogan is 'Listen,' one may hope that the theorist is on the way to catch up with his subject, a goal seldom reached in musical history."

## GLOSSARY OF MODERN TERMINOLOGY

ATONALITY—Regarded by some as the ideal of a music without key center; and by others, music with uncertain key basis or changing key center.

DISSONANT COUNTERPOINT—The new counterpoint in which dissonances are brought into more direct contact than in strict consonant counterpoint.

DUODECUPLE SCALE—A twelve-note scale, usually without definite tonality, used by atonal writers. A combination of two whole-tone scales semitonally associated.

LINEAR COUNTERPOINT—An adaptation of the old tonal counterpoint to the altered demands of the new "supertonal" harmony. Melodic lines combined in unorthodox counterpoint with atonal relations.

POLYTONALITY—The result of the simultaneous use of more than one tonality.

POLYCHORD—The simultaneous use of two chords of varying tonalities.

POLYHARMONY—A succession of polychords welded together with the idea of an agreeable musical relationship. The relation is usually polytonal but may be diatonic only.

WHOLE-TONE SCALES—Atonal scales arranged by whole-steps. One half of a duodecuple scale.

SUPERDOMINANT—An enlarged dominant which includes additional overtones from the harmonic series, tones whose use is made possible by the chromatic resolution of the parts, and only acceptable because of the notes additional to the final tonic.

WHOLE-TONE DOMINANT—A dominant chord which contains all notes of the whole-tone scale, i.e., including the augmented eleventh and minor thirteenth, and with the fifth omitted, or divided (raised and lowered simultaneously).

# INDEX